High Shelf

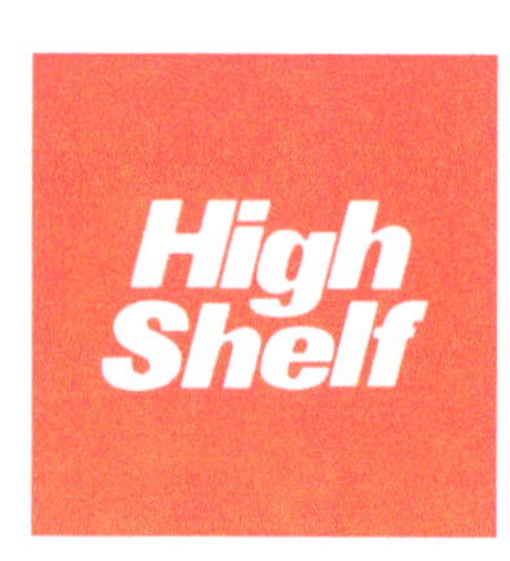

High Shelf XXXVIII. January 2022.
Portland, Oregon.
Copyright 2022, High Shelf Press

ISBN: 978-1-952869-53-2

Cover Image by D.T. Graber
Editing, Design and Layout by C. M. Tollefson

With special thanks to:
David Seung & Eric Hoskins

High Shelf XXXVIII

January 2022

"Dying man can't get his want into words
but that doesn't deter want, does it… "
George Yatchisin

"... The closer we get to deciphering the zodiac, the faster it disappears.
Dim bulb made dumber the brighter we shine, exhausting

one life at a time naming each thing before it winks out.
I am an echo drifting back to myself drinking air that swarms the trees ..."
Shyla Shehan

Table Of Contents

Birthday

A. Pikovsky

today i mourned.

oh, the vines of my youth
so twisted & blistered
& plastered.

like twigs of the tree—just strangled.
fallen figs: among the broken wasp wings
just dried, then torn.

oh, the despair of my internal king—& another (!!!)
birthday caked
 in distraction.

little corners patched in suffering
you blew on white bulbs
& i remembered the petals used to be yellow.

Palm against palm,
i found my mind in the center of a ditch
& in the midst of stridulating,
we entered spring.

oh, the tannins of ((my)) hemmed exploration!
it's where i learned to walk
beneath the coals
baking in the focused depth of your soothing pitch.

Desert Oasis

D.T. Graber

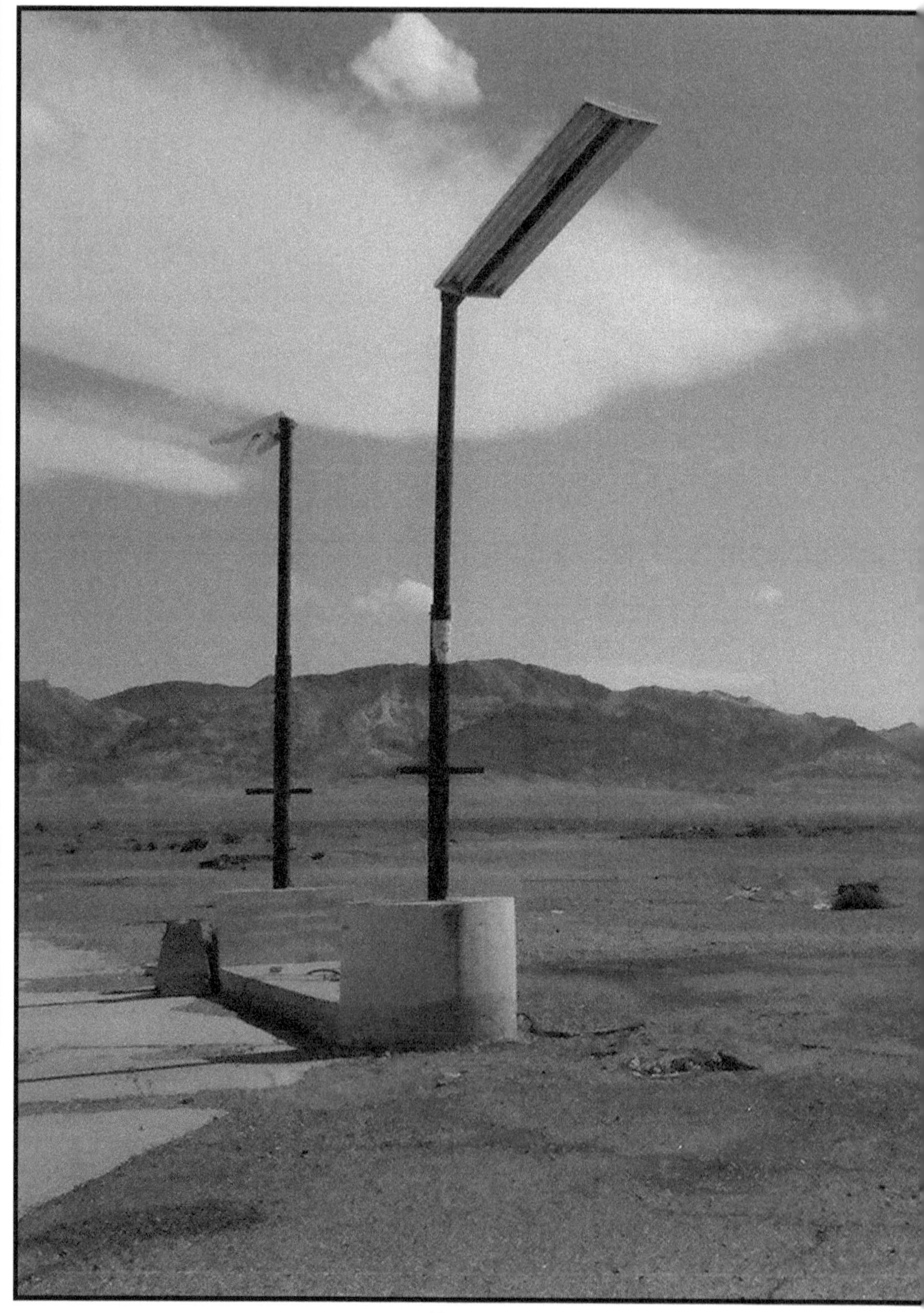

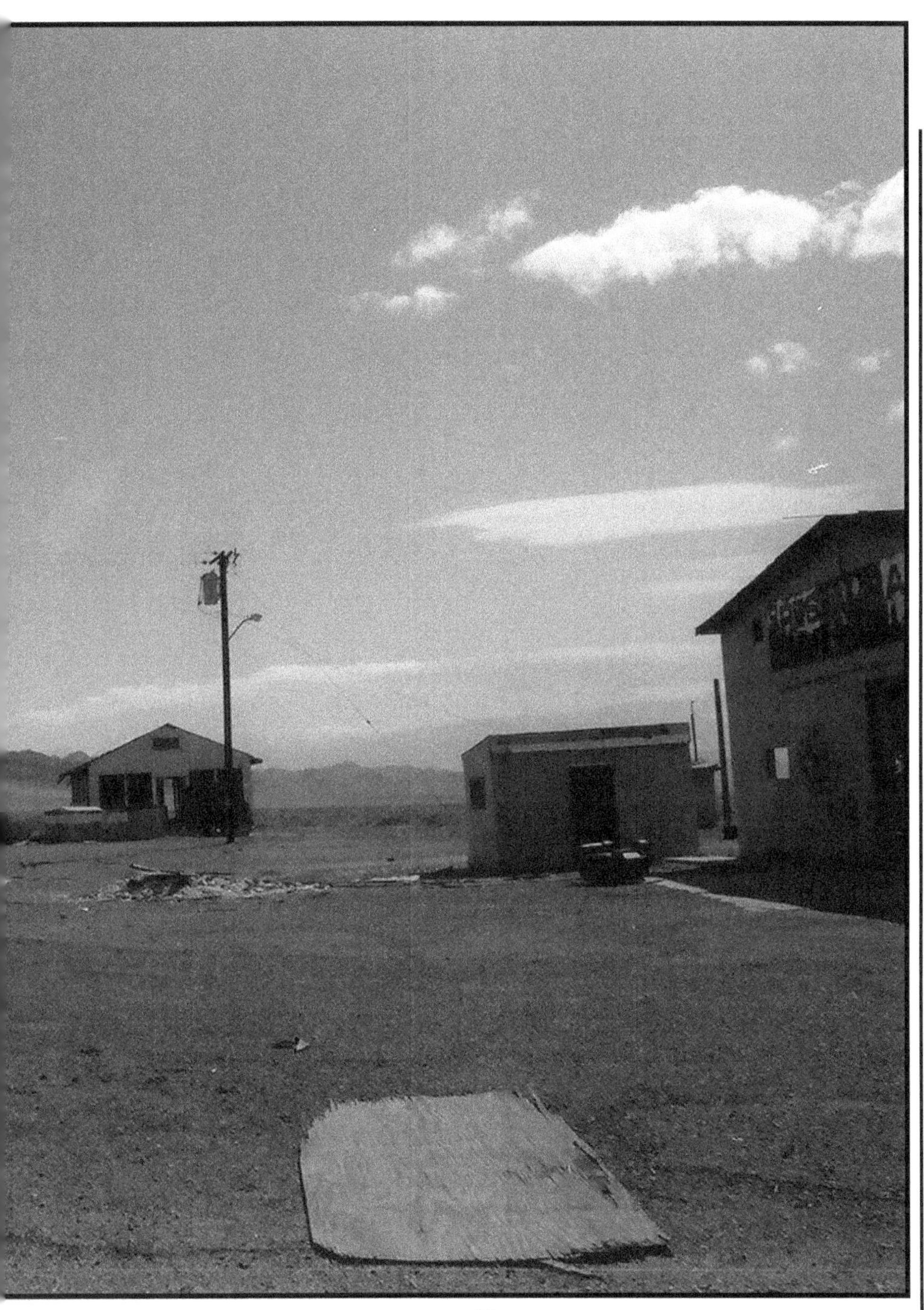

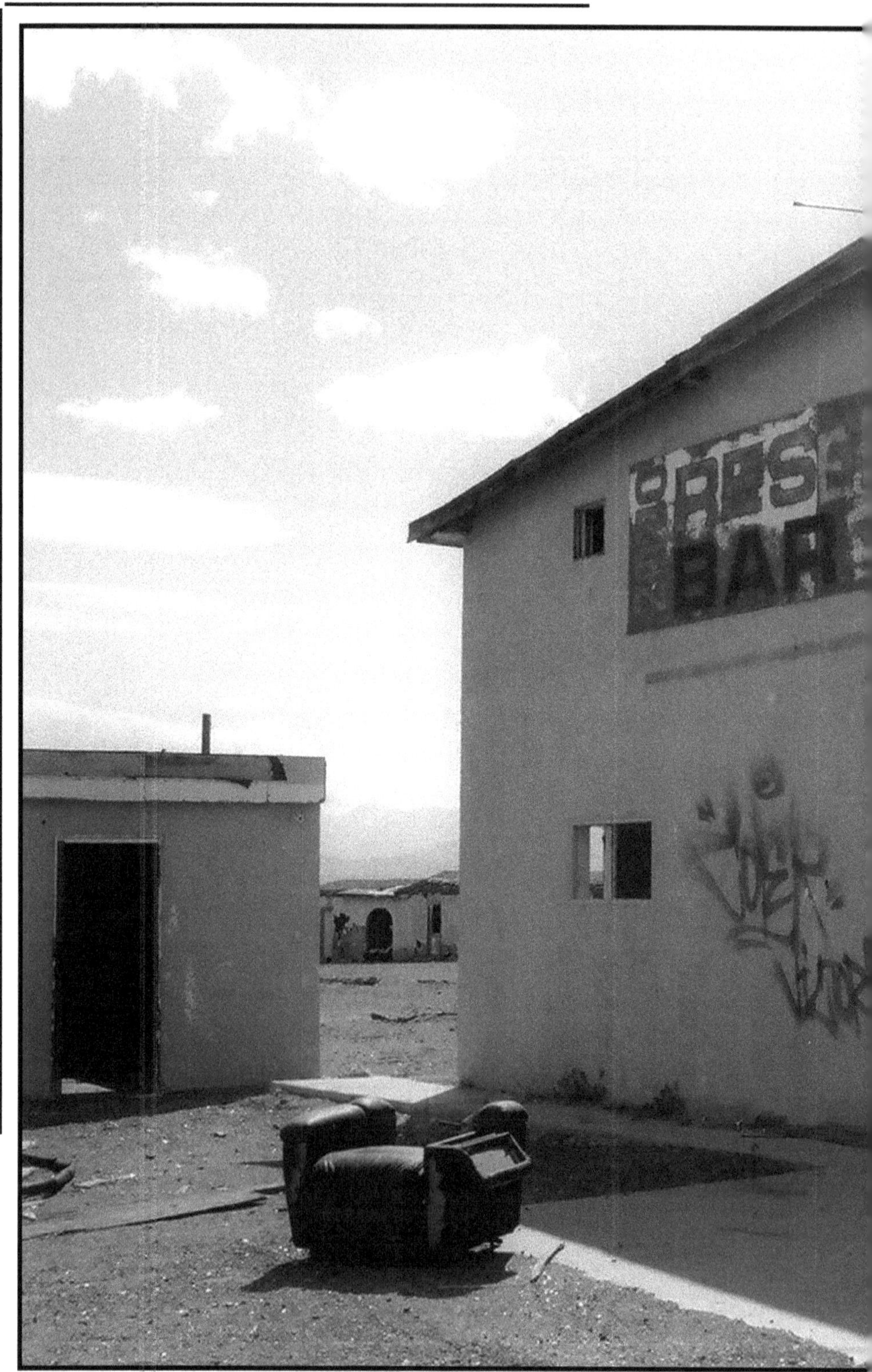

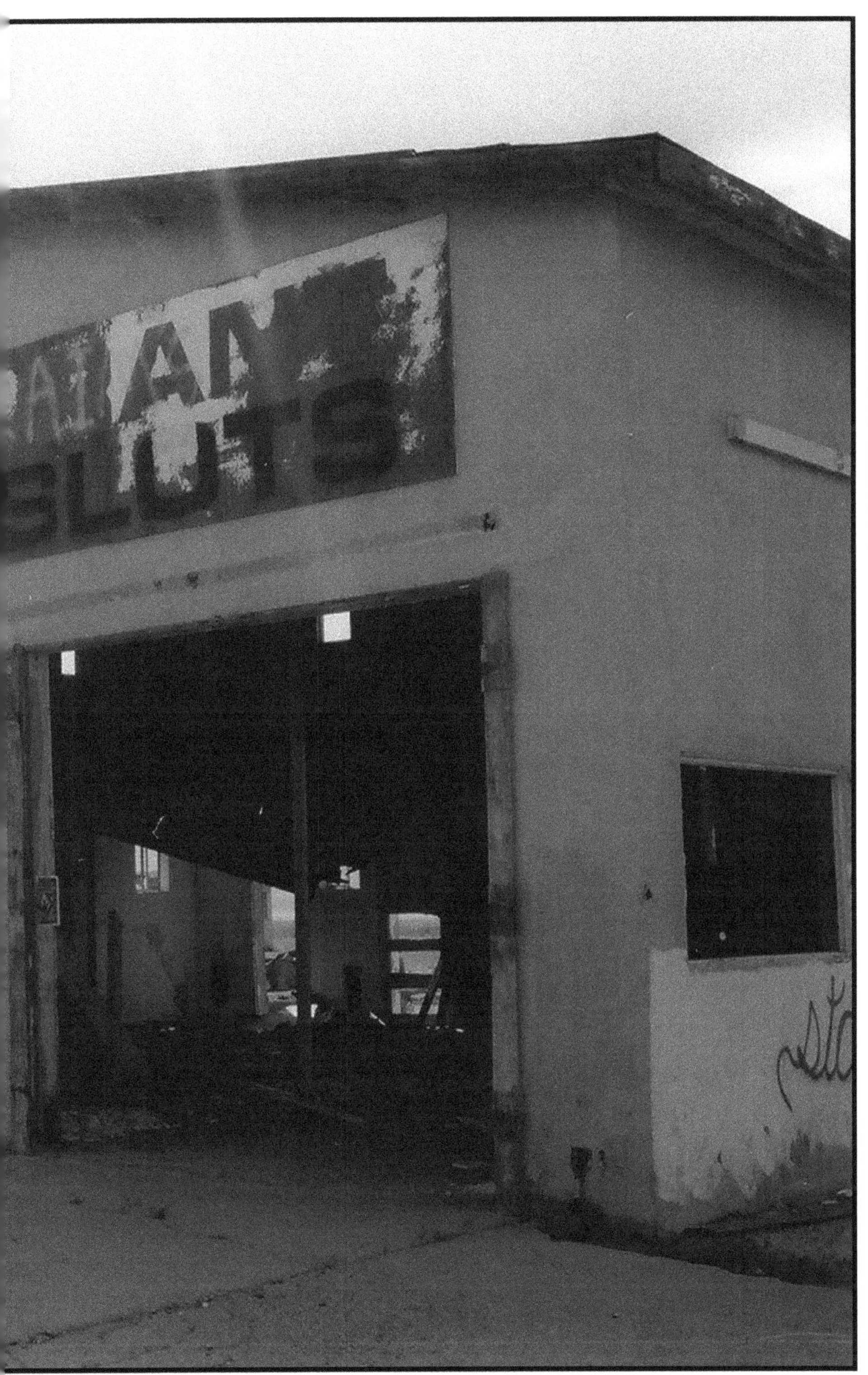

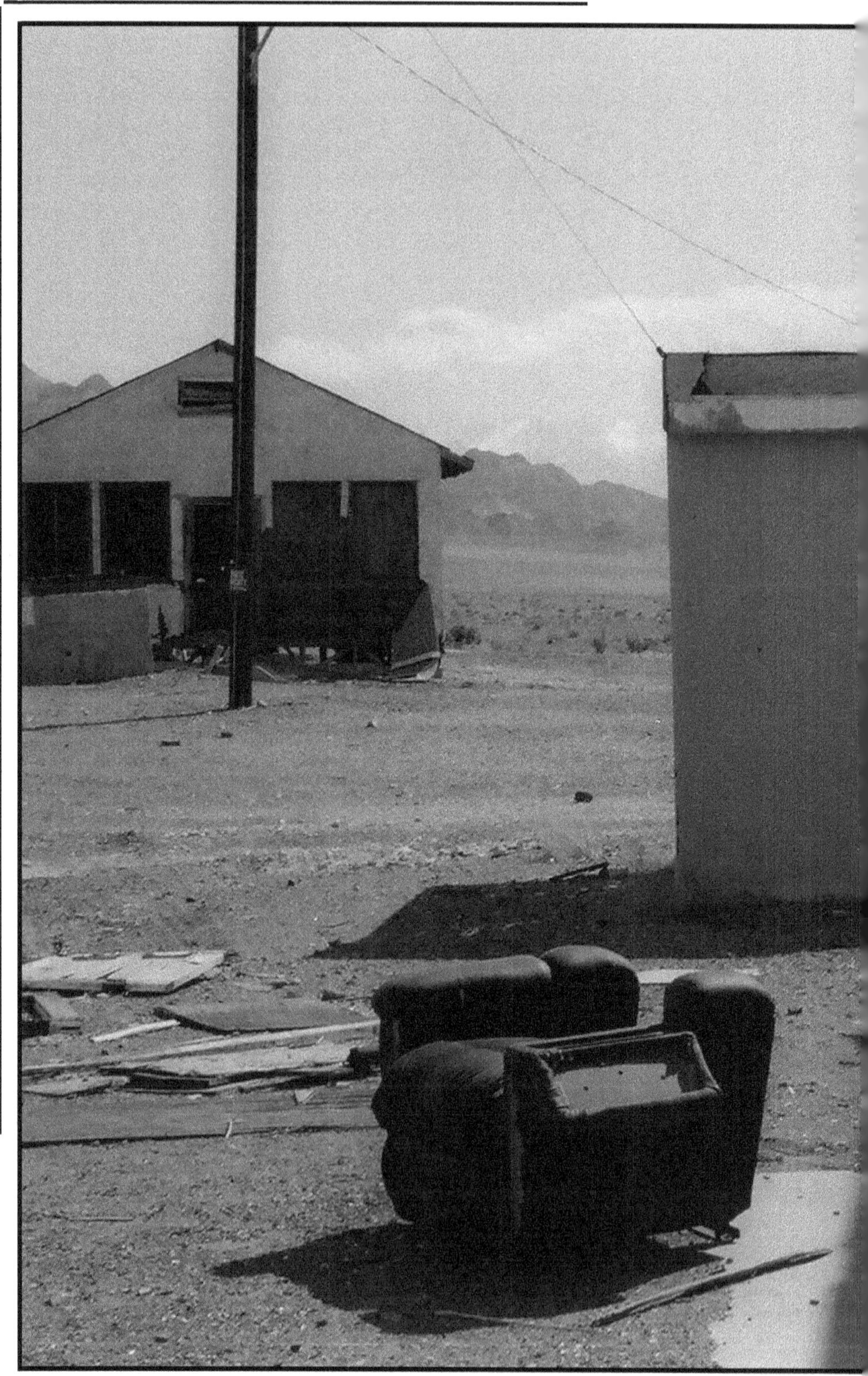

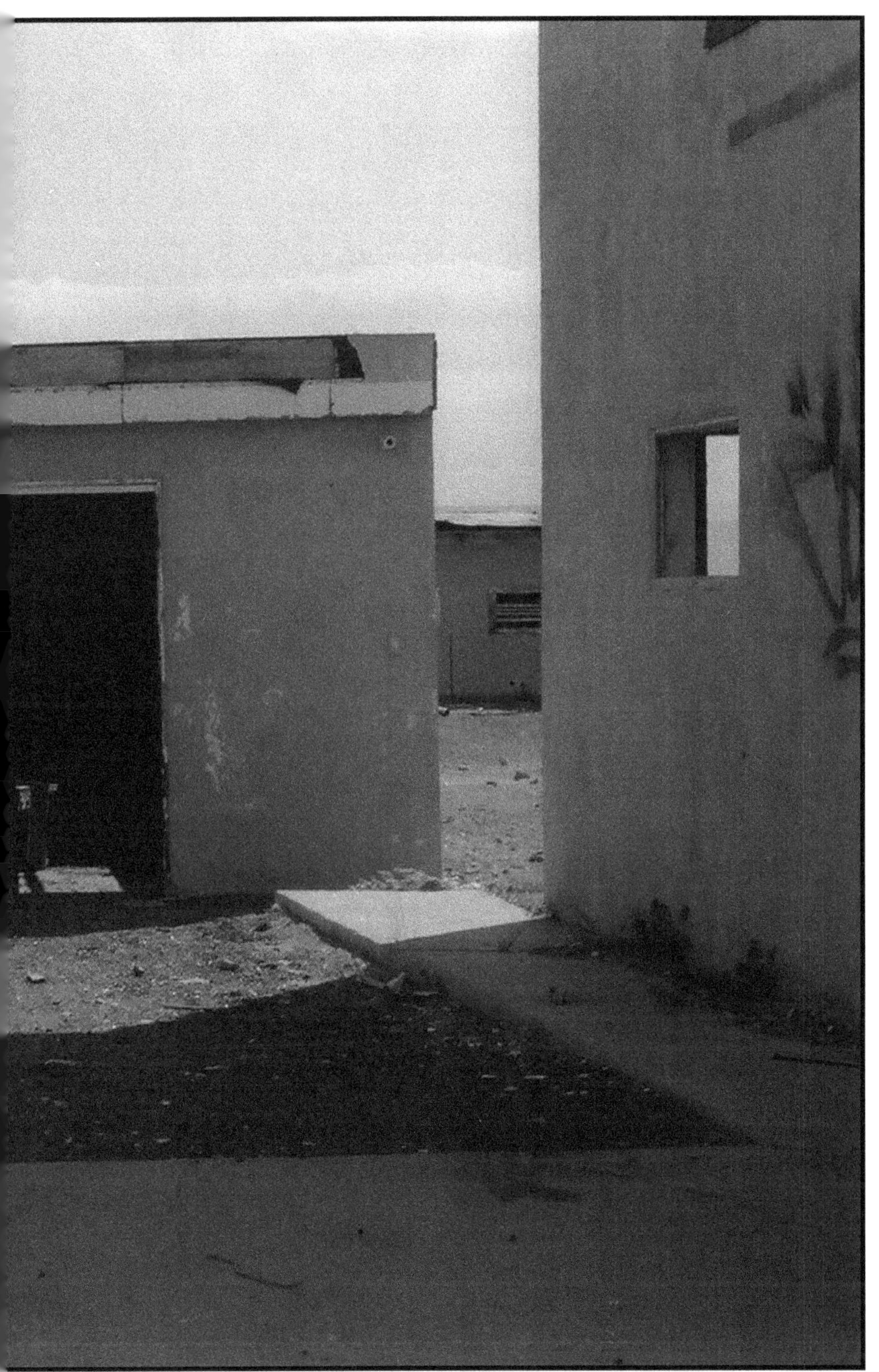

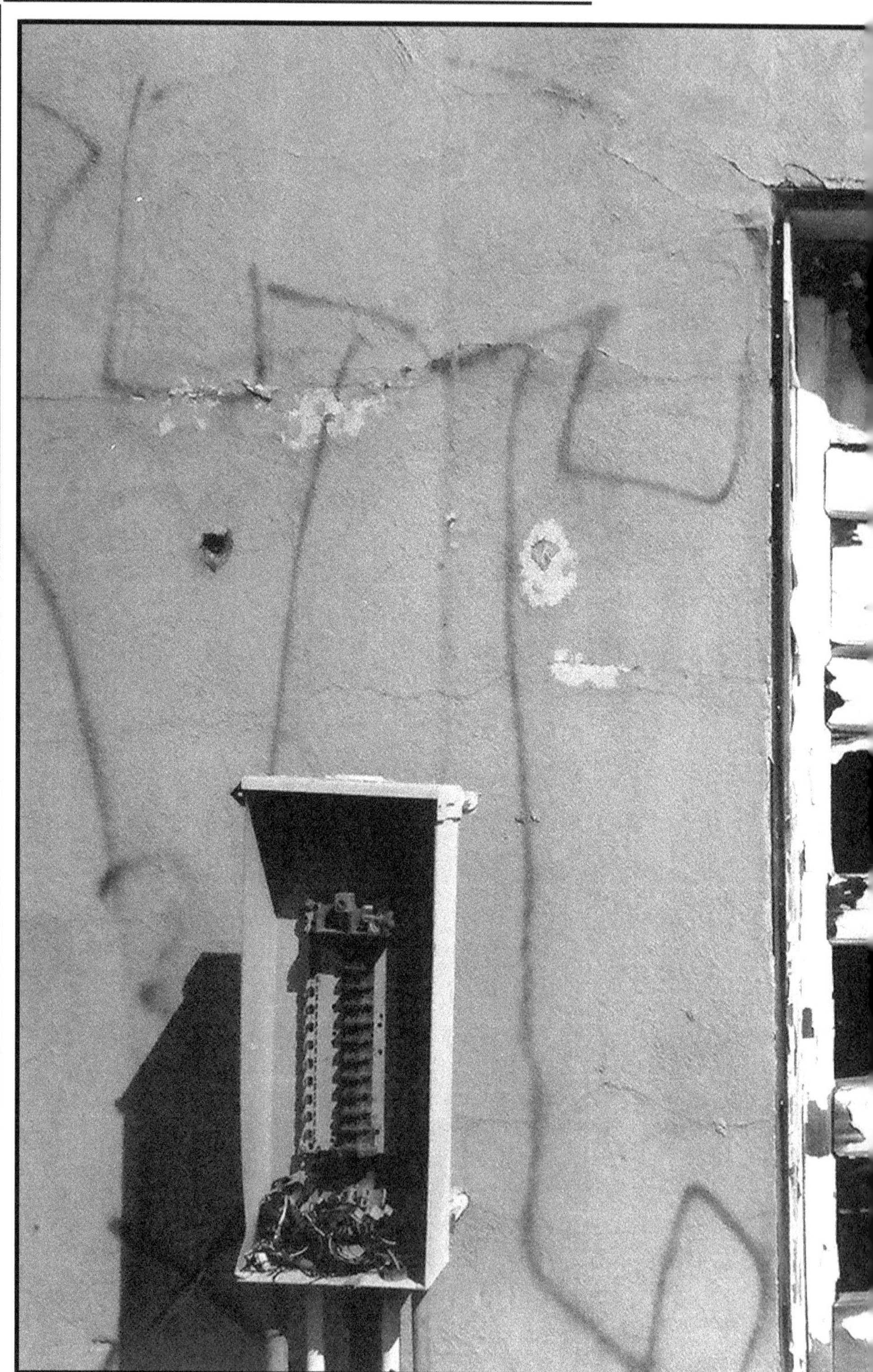

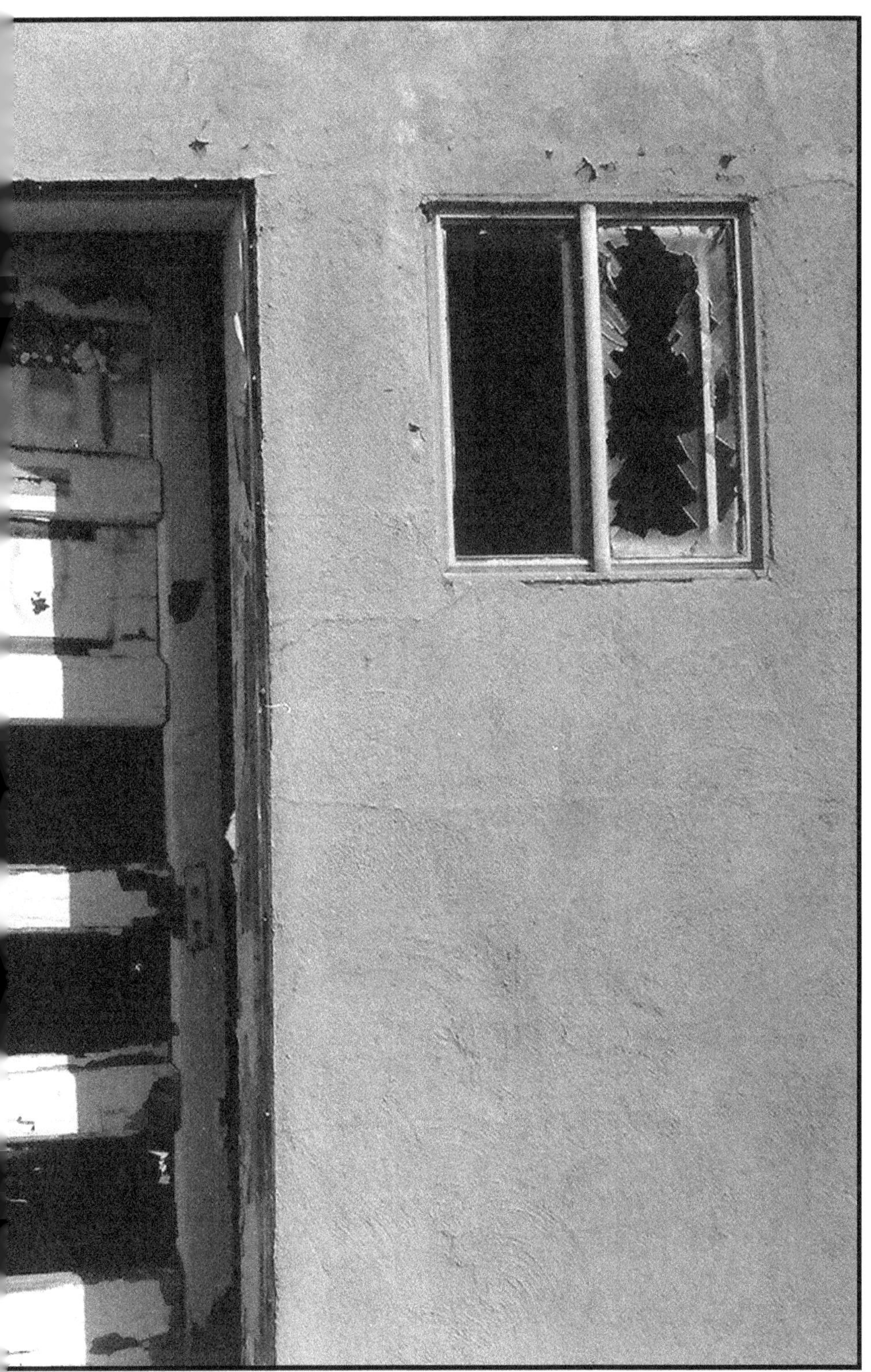

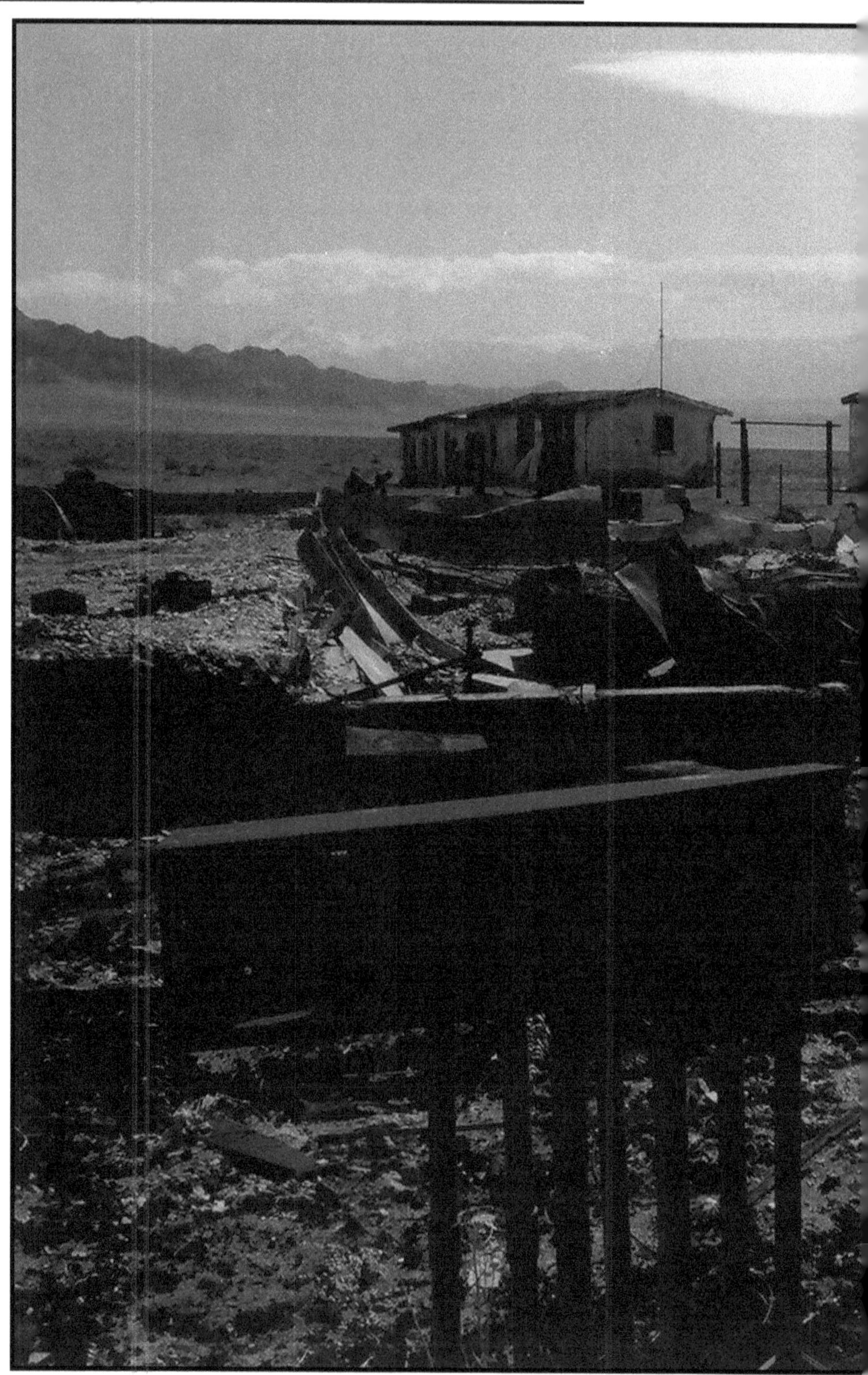

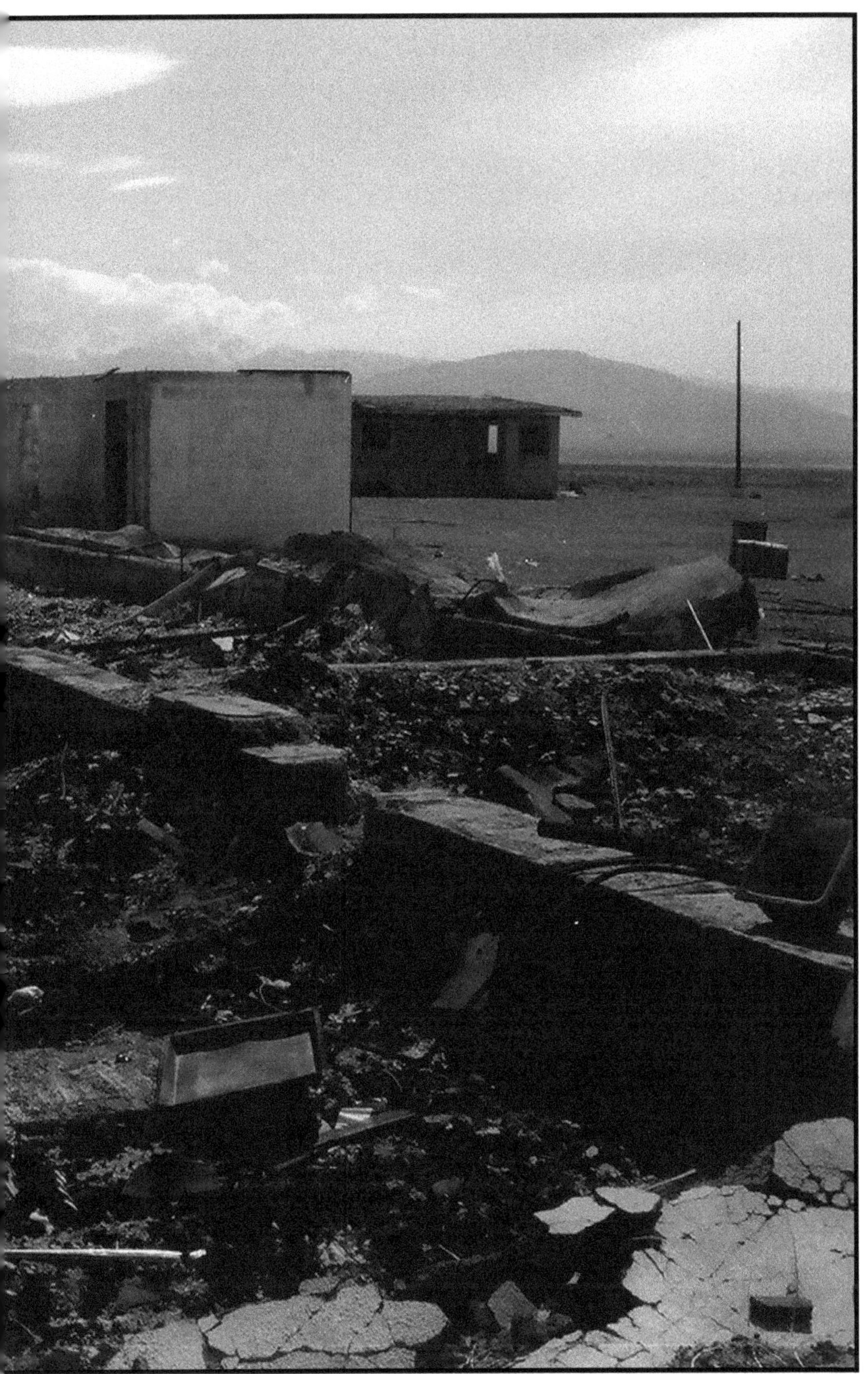

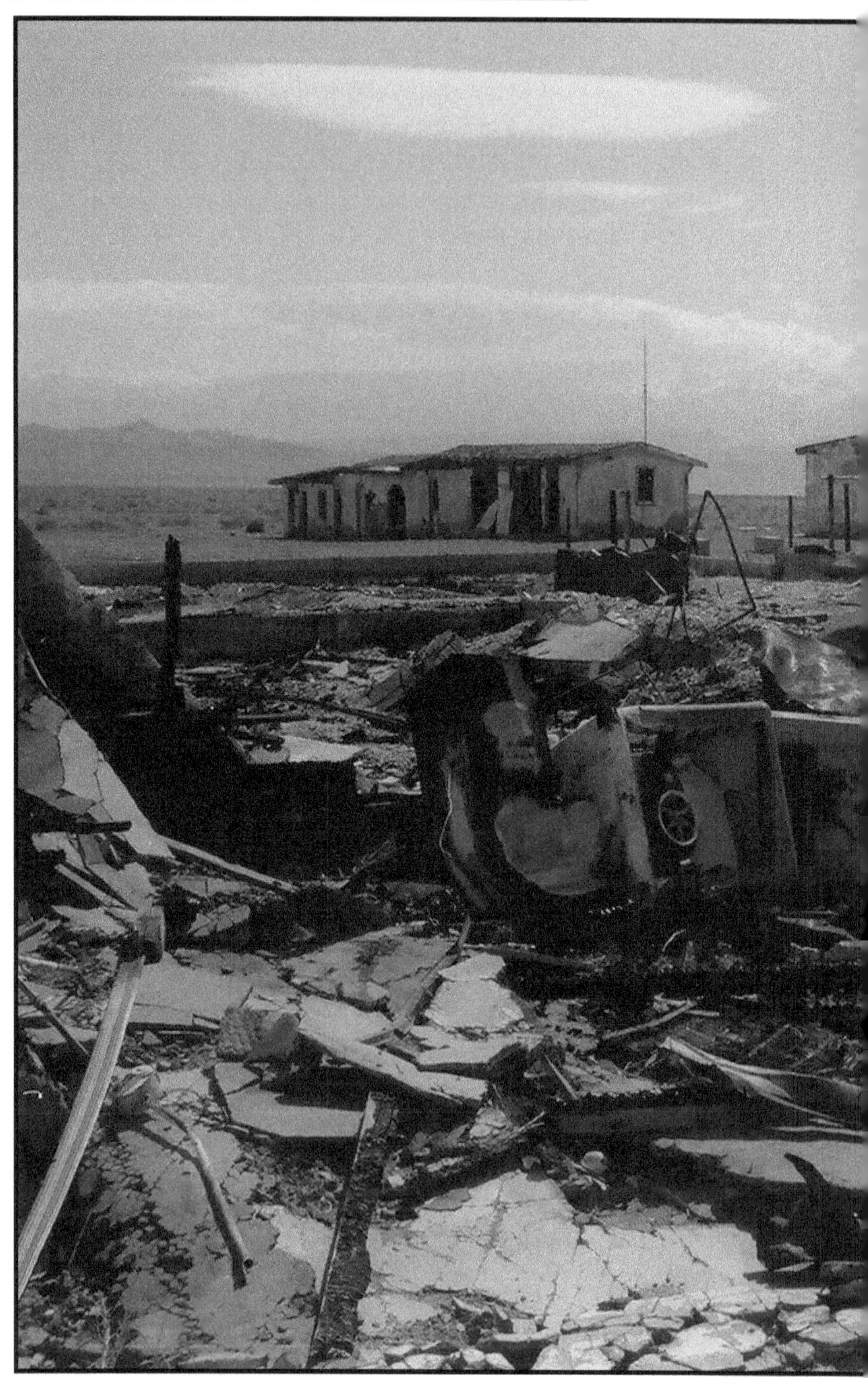

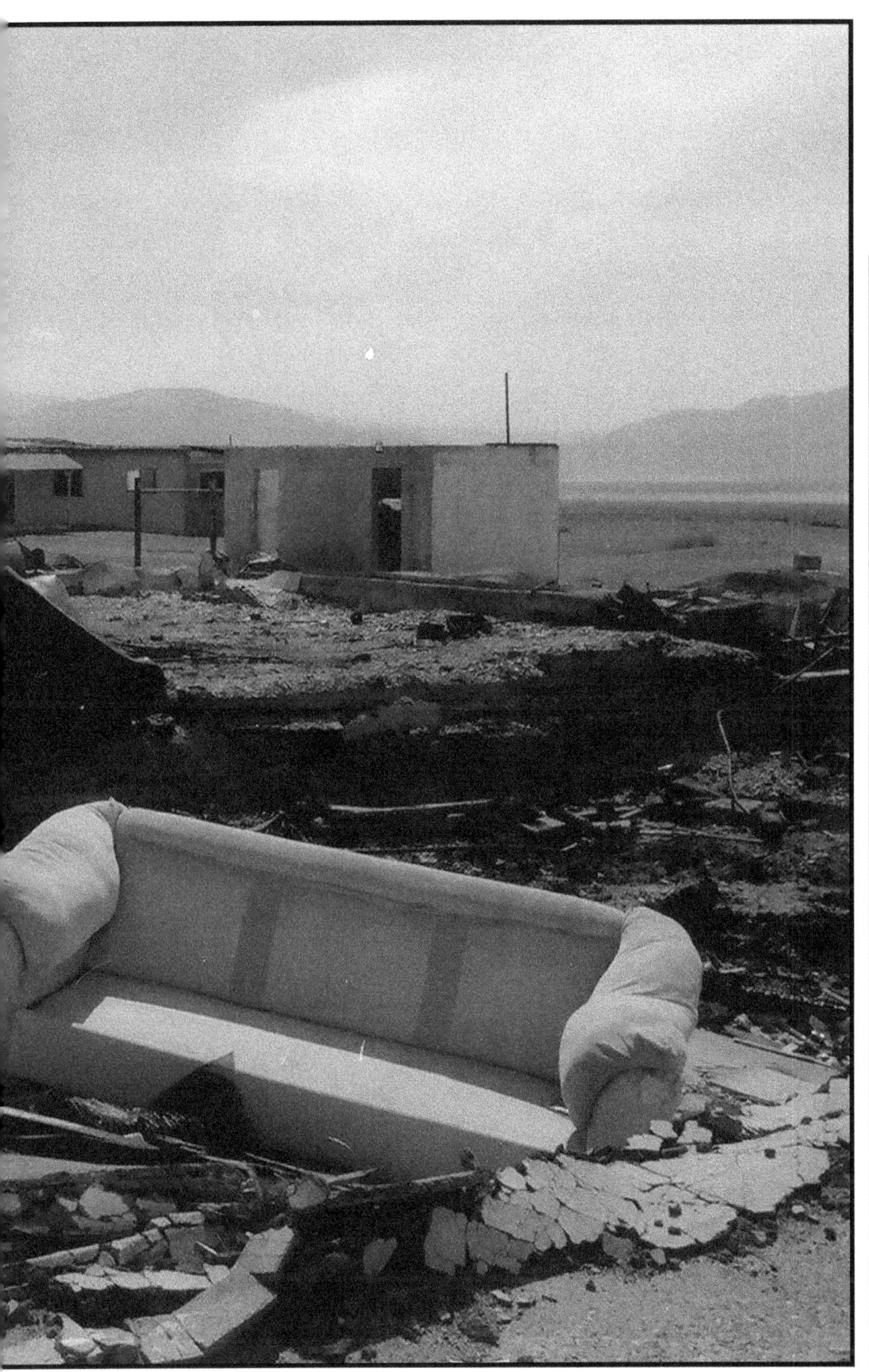

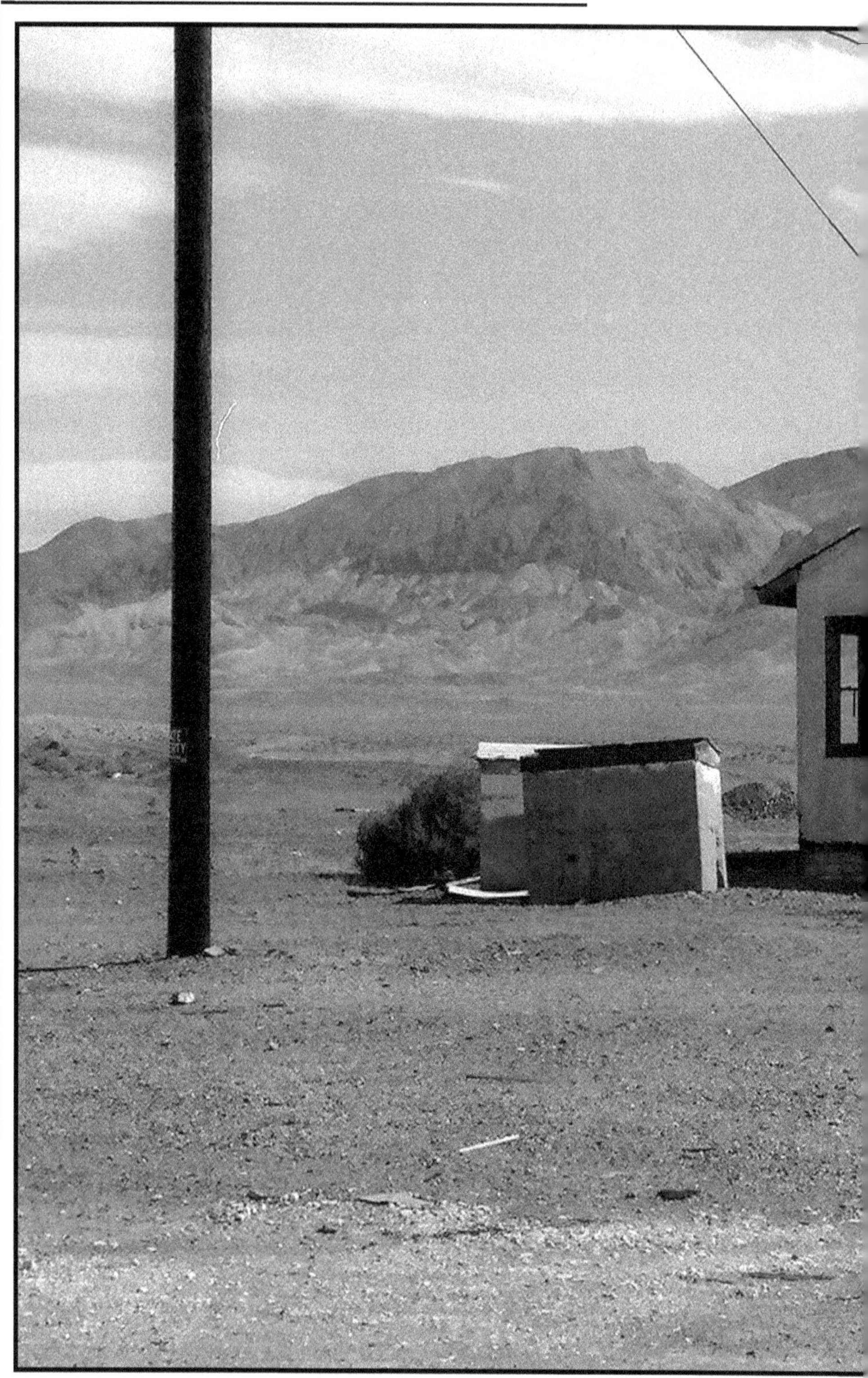

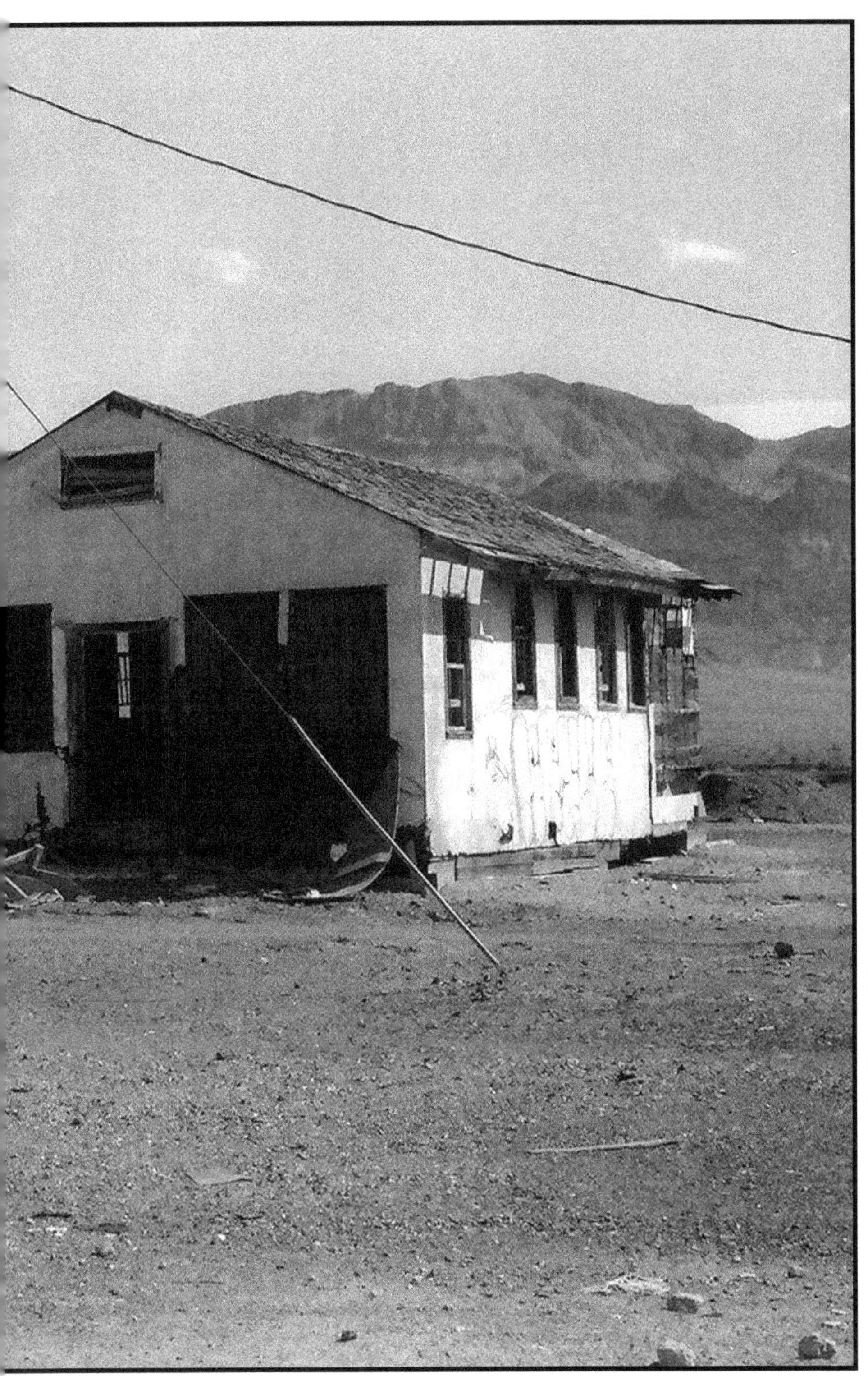

Evening of the second attempt

Brian Baker

Before the violet violence began:

headed home, earlier in the evening, suddenly
against floods come up from beneath asphalt,
upstream I went against the river of it,
black and spreading itself out around
each cross-street, billowing up
against concrete continents, out
of place and of unknown origin

until the accident
comes slowly to me, another vehicle
at odd angle to the roadway, the pavement
itself caved in, weakened finally
by the burst pipe in its heart,
accepting this offering of metal
and torn rubber, flowing out
its thanks around it, finally free of the pressure,
given itself up to slope and gravity,
searching out entry, then wild in
the storm sewers, gone
in all directions.

Later on, though, after the call,
returning downtown,
and passing this spot again,
maneuvering the lights and barriers

but this time am only preoccupied with how and why
her body surrounds pills so easily
and completely, no matter their number,
strength or purpose. In between the
curtains, lights, and all the reasons,
someone's voice saying *I love you*
as it hovers there, trapped among
the wires and tubes and blips on screens.

After this, needing to find someplace
to wait for results, we are
outside of this building, looking up as
the midnight sky turns violet

in intervals. The heat builds up
north of here, disperses white-hot
where it is. Turns violet, though,
in the miles between us, does this
with a murmur, does this
with a warning.

Waiting, because of it,
for many *kinds* of results---
the ones of blood-work,
the ones of high electricity
and heat exchange, the ones
of damage.

Much like the first time, though,
nothing has changed.
They say she is as safe
as we knew she would be,
the others who waited with me
are finally loosed in
different directions
and mine, now, means
home.

So for the third time
I pass the accident scene,
concerned with nothing else now
but the details of it.

Men have stopped the bleeding,
have sought out and found
the ruptured line and so much tearing done
in doing so.
Only their heads can be seen
as they stand upon the vein,
lowering in its replacement,
spare parts doing the work
the old ones no longer can

except that no amount of patchwork
cures completely, we leave behind
something which has been repaired

but then, at another moment
(between the white-hot

and the violet)
the rains may fall heavily again, storms creep about
the area around us, threatening
to overload what systems there are
beneath human skin

and the harder skin
men manufacture.

Everything That Rises Must Submerge

George Yatchisin

Dying man can't get his want into words
but that doesn't deter want, does it,
his moans a call, a question, need
kneaded into a ball of dough no one
cares to eat—that bitter salt,
a crust that cuts.
                    You hope to help
but there's nothing more pitiful than that,
like a stormy sky lit dazzlingly gray
while it gathers its forces between pours.
Locate the oxygen tube. Clip near the nose.
Loop the doubled hose over each ear.
Elevate the electric bed until what's left
of the fire in his eyes quiets. Silence, then,
a gratitude that floods the sick room. Go
Noah on your boat to a new clean world.

Fever-dream August

Chris Norcross

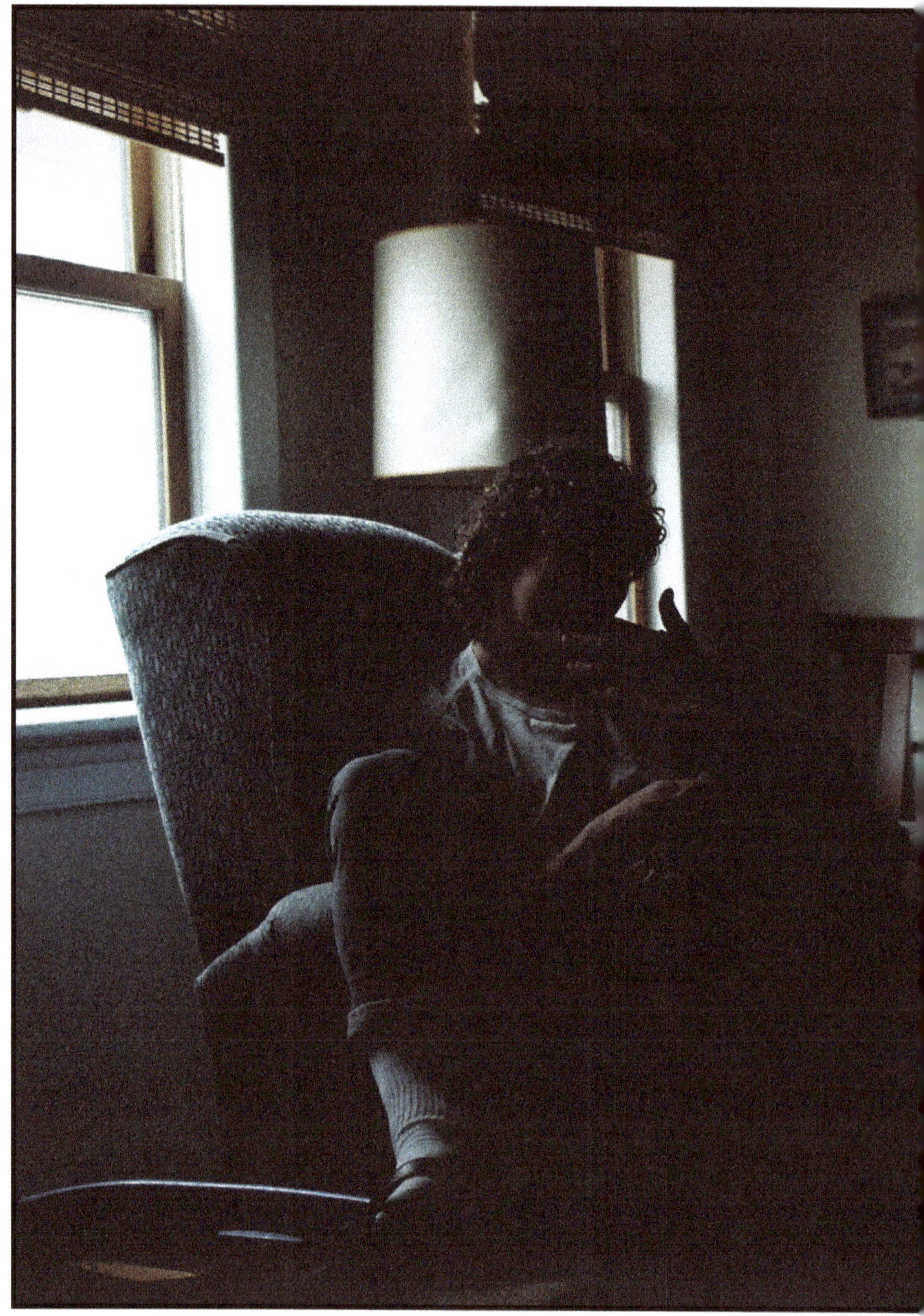

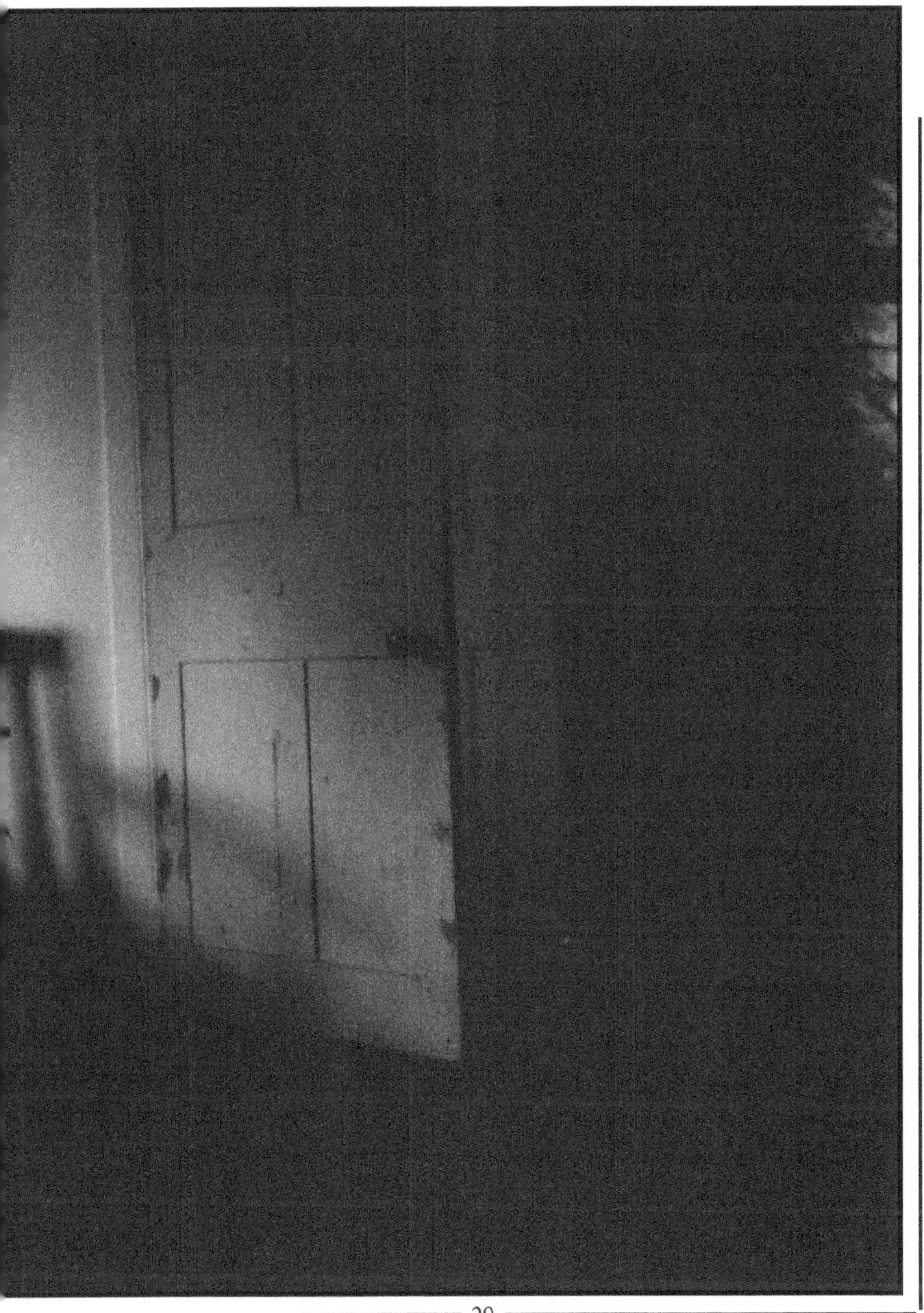

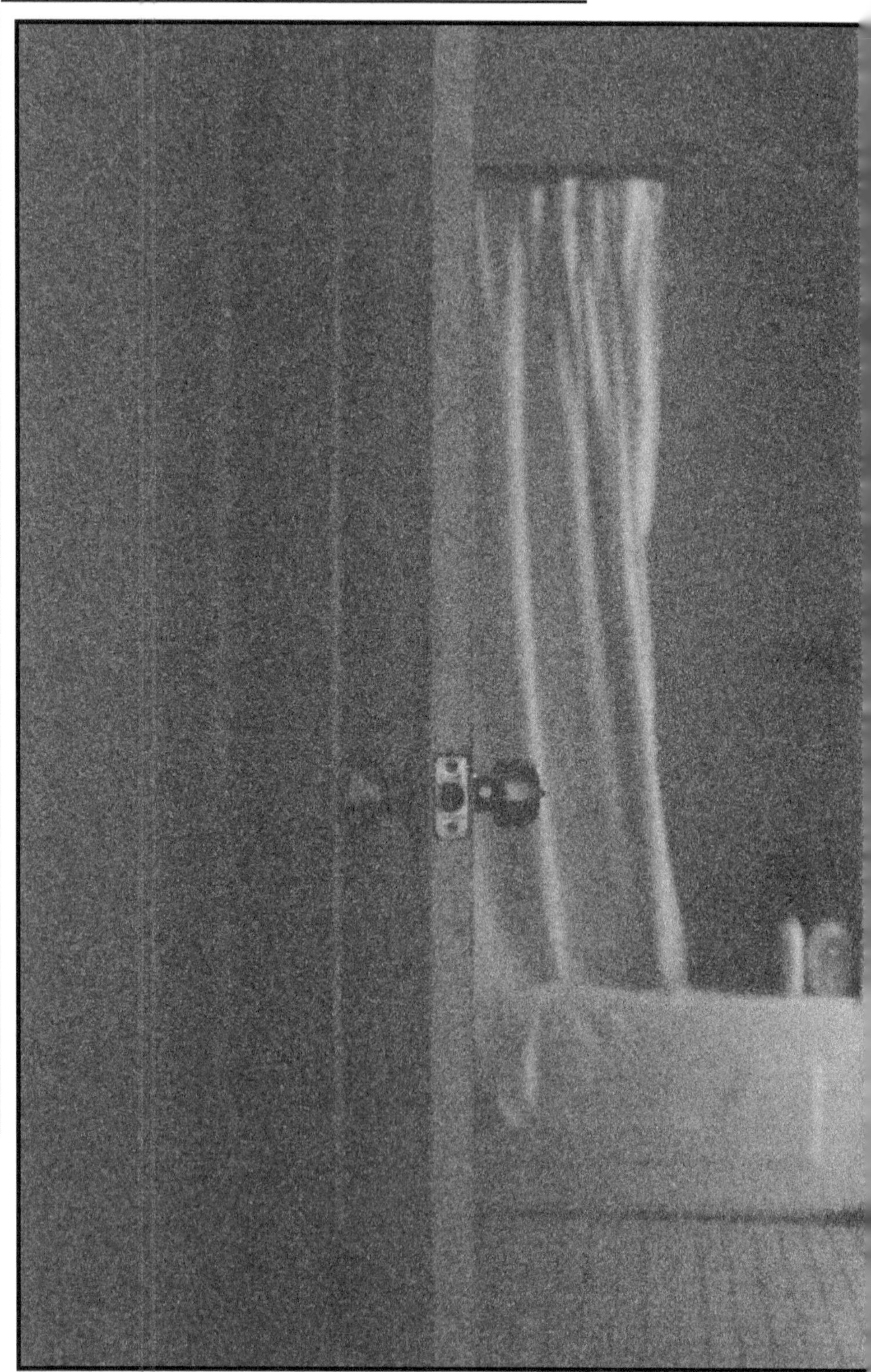

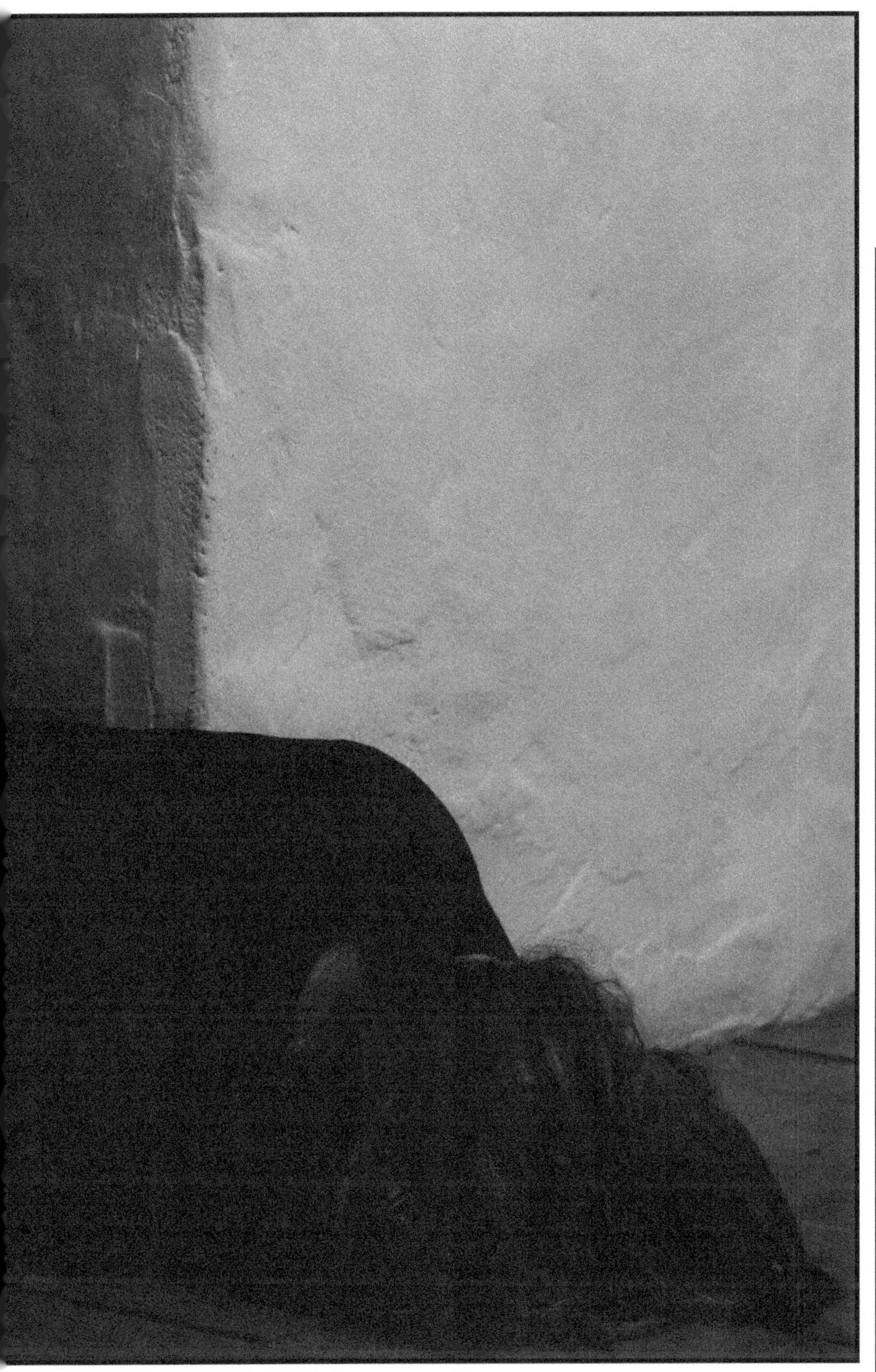

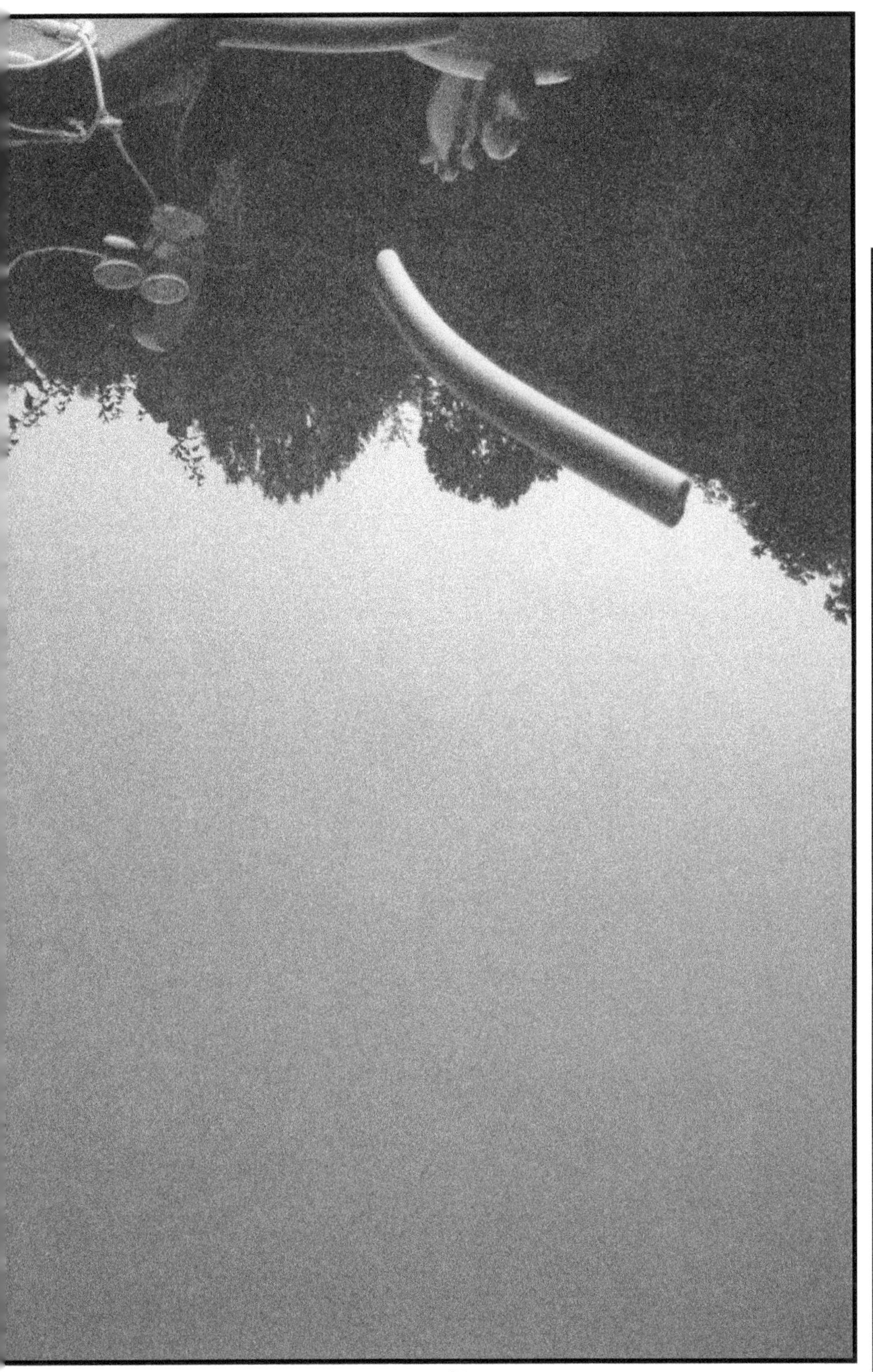

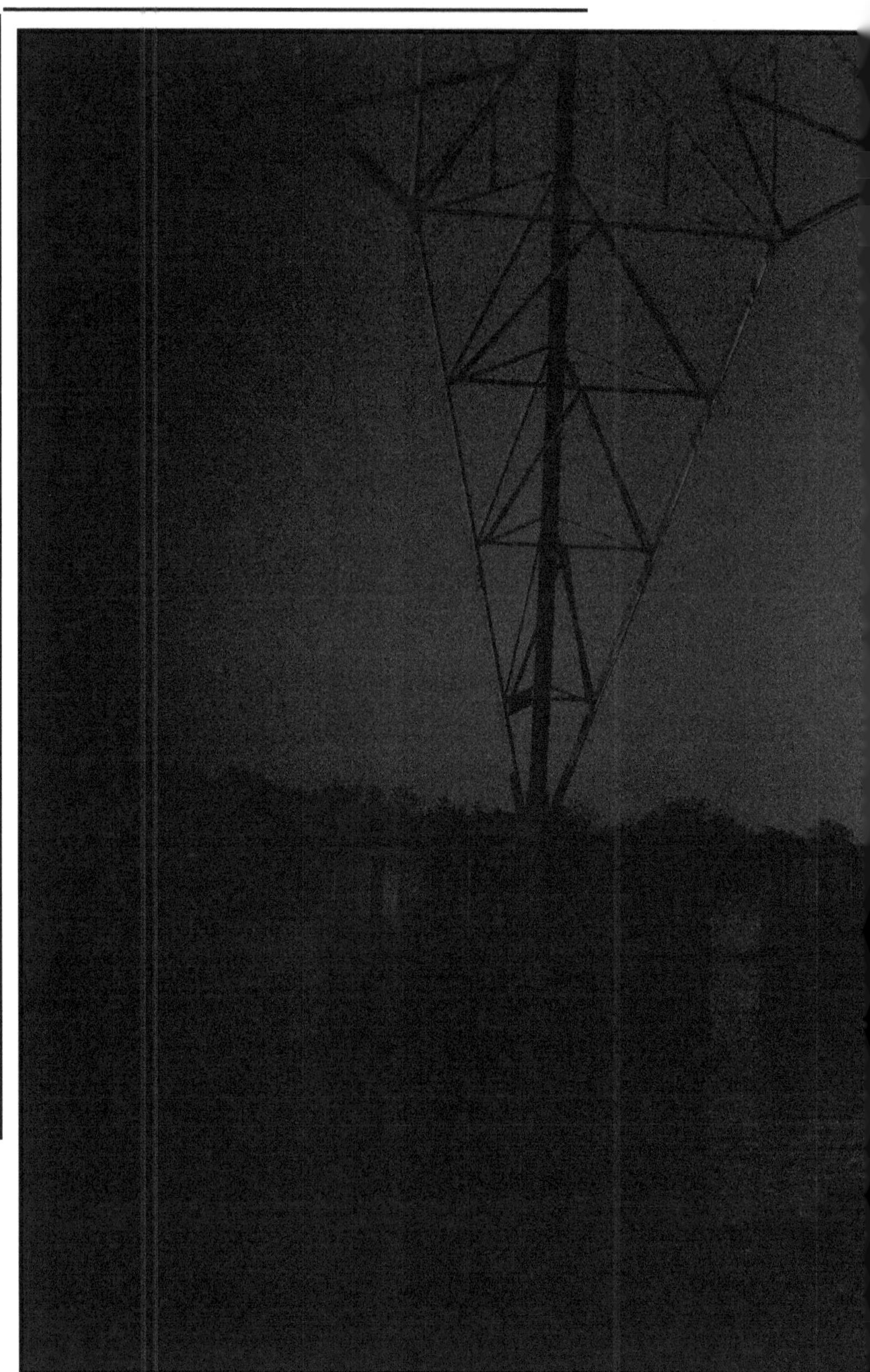

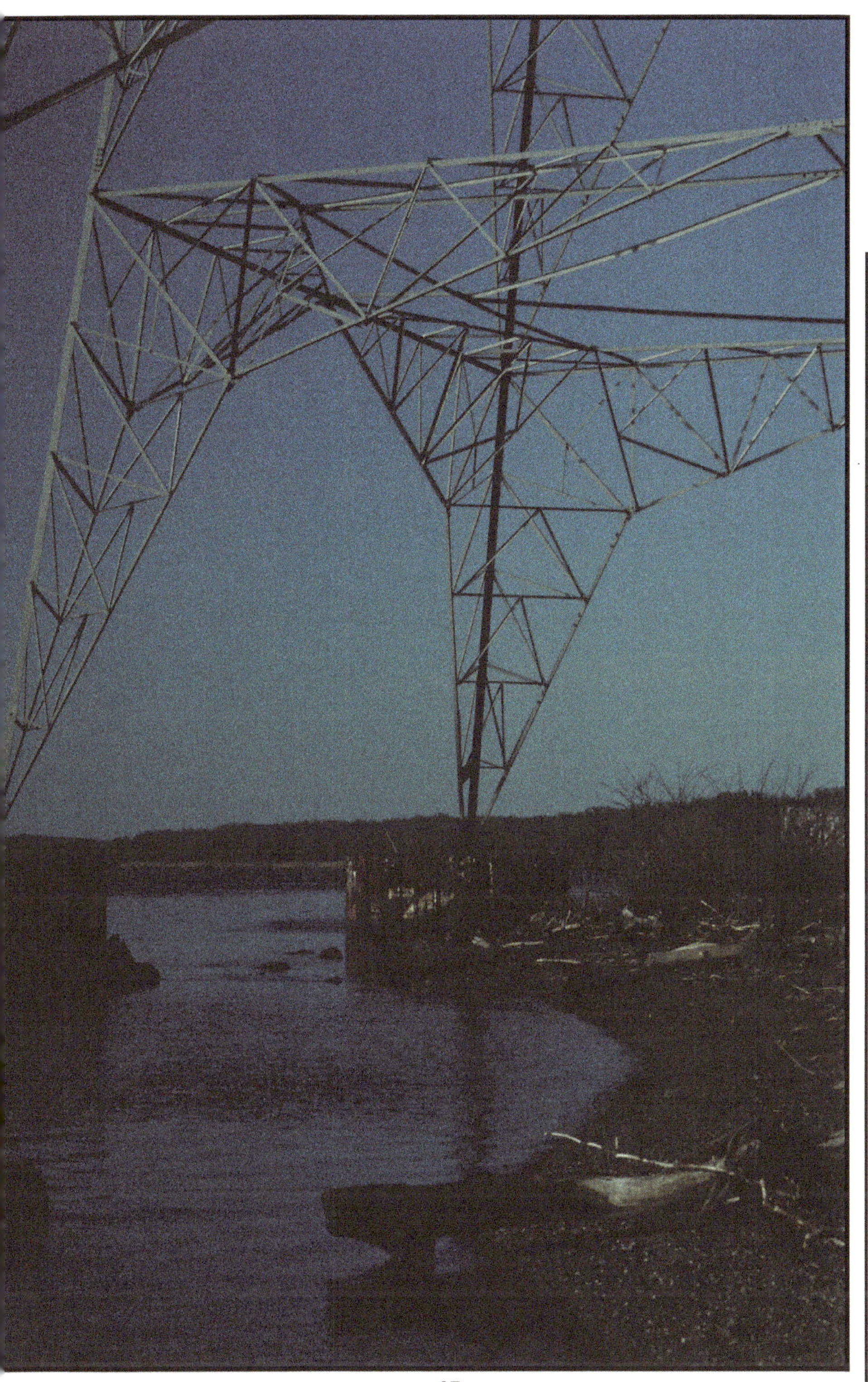

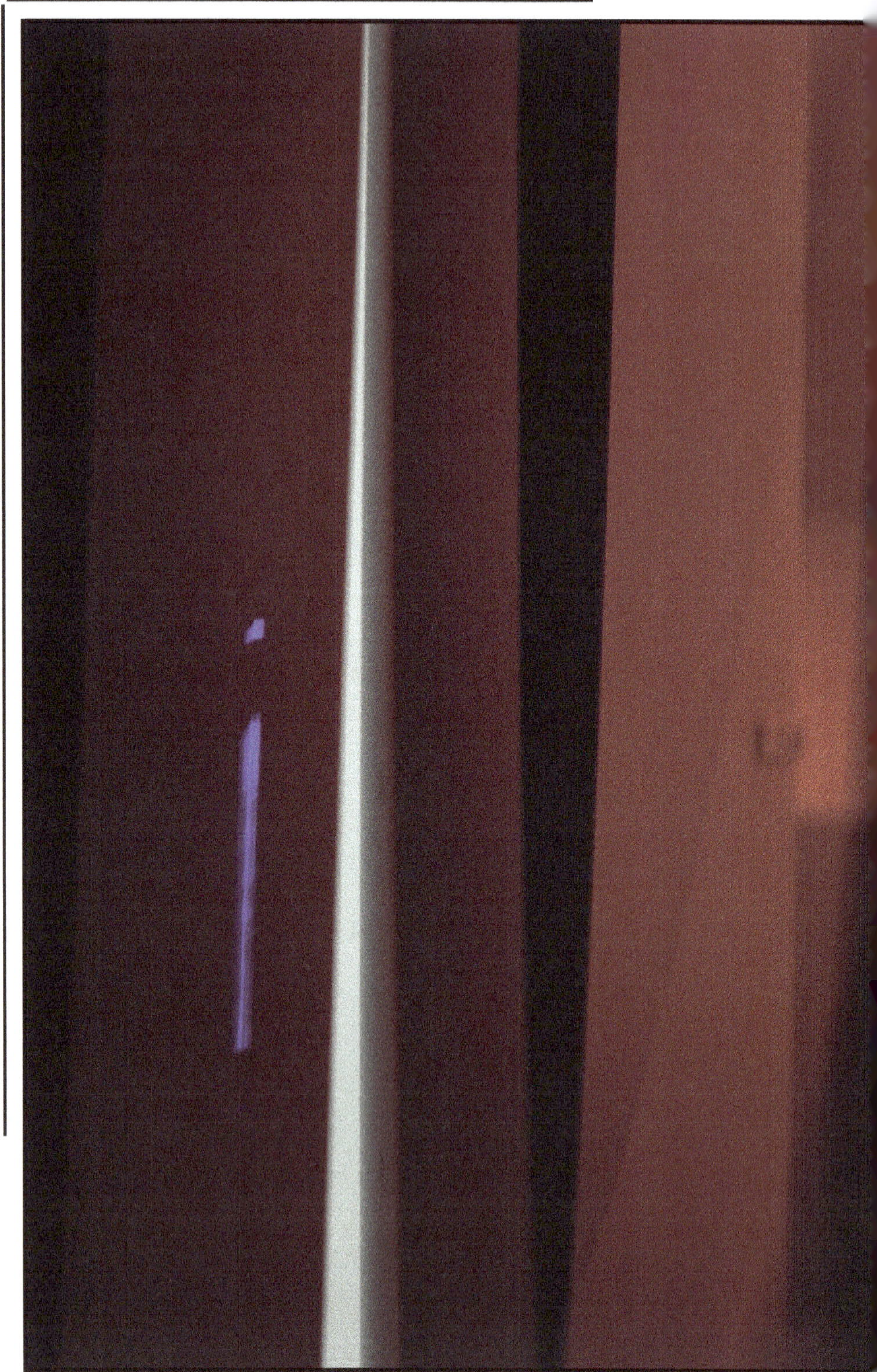

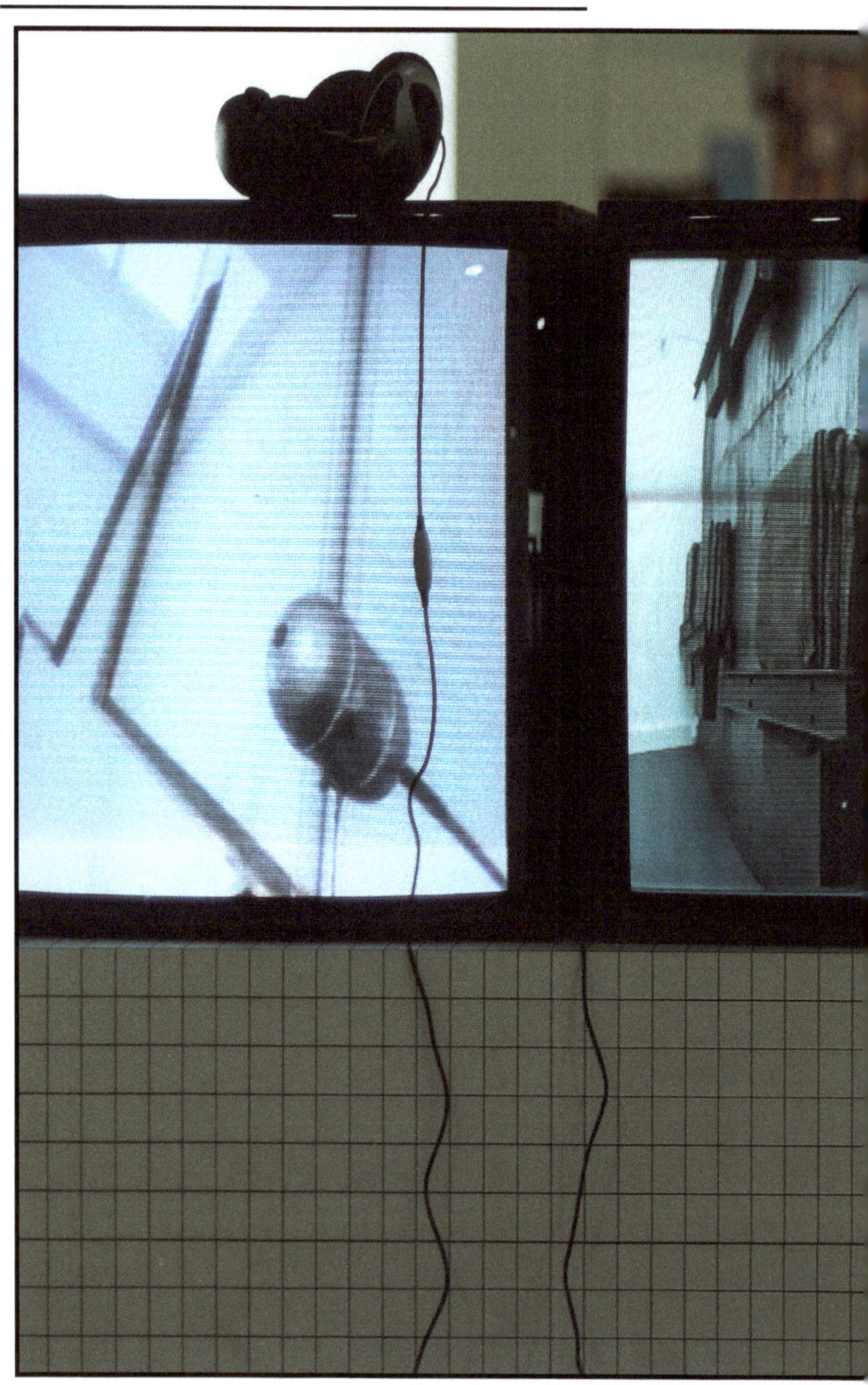

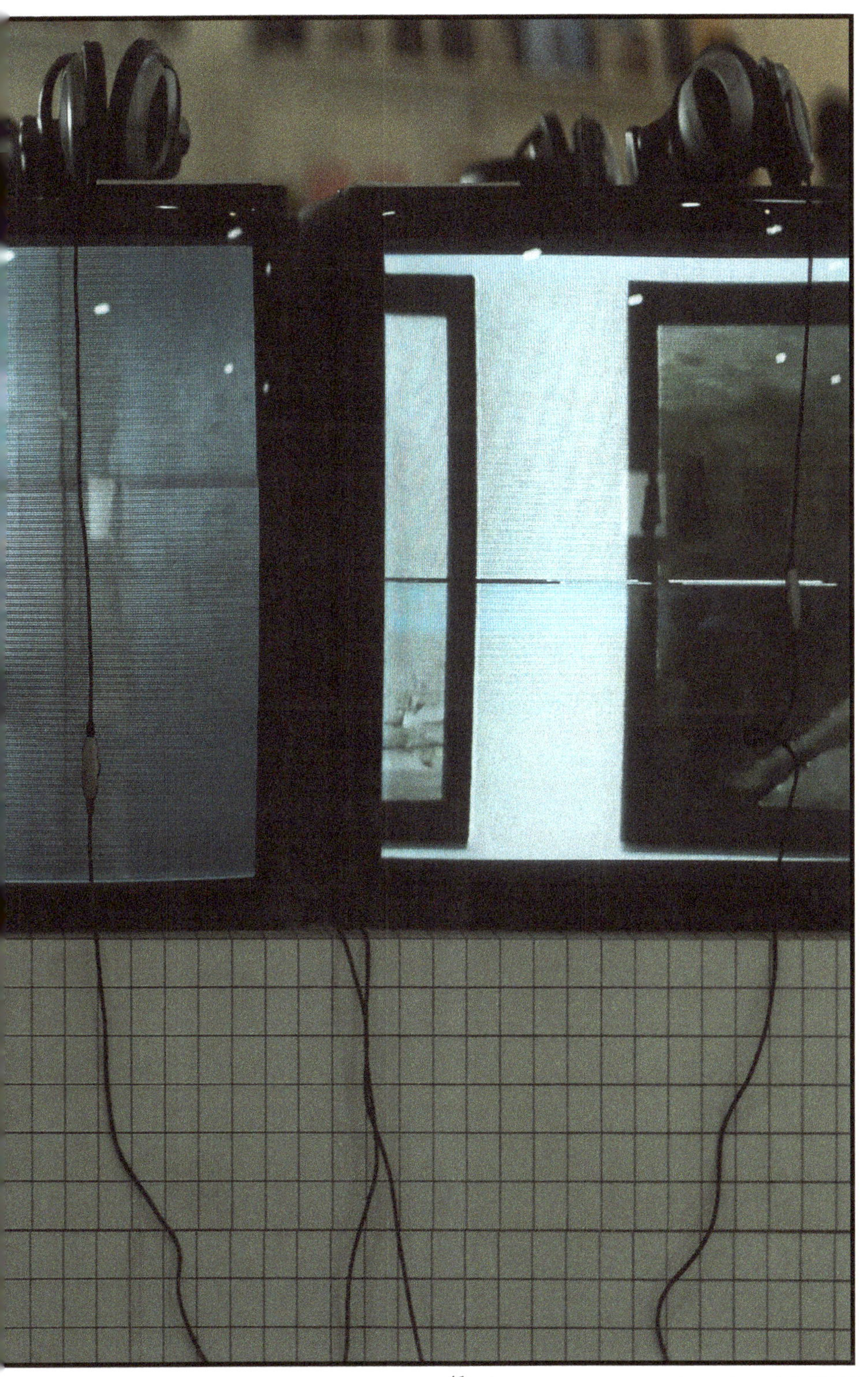

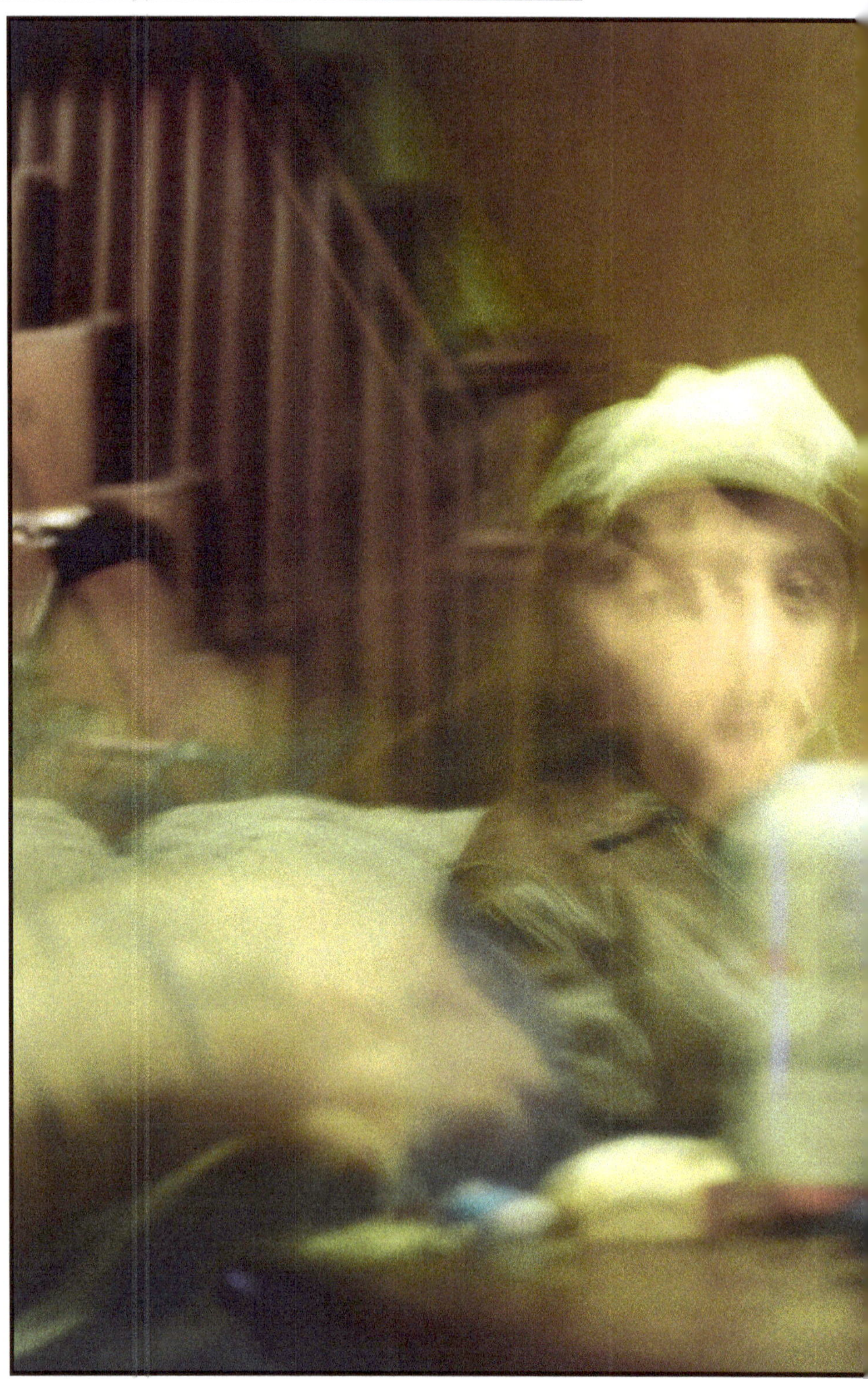

Here's My Playbook

Dion Farquhar

> ...the case of poor servants was very dismal....
> —Daniel Defoe, *Journal of the Plague Year*

Poor fools, you're in love

with those you've lost

you wallow and mourn

whereas my metrics

mine the bottom line:

my survival's just

a glitch in the code

productive, efficient

feelings-free calculator

like your own abstracted Oppenheimer

in the Los Alamos desert:

(translating his own Sanskrit)

I am become death, destroyer of worlds

economies of scale work best:

why waste time with the robust, the young?

the most vulnerable the best bet

those jammed together:

try the favelas—Rio, Sao Paolo

for the U.S.—the black belt

of Alabama

the bloody abattoirs of the Midwest

—illegals don't dare complain—

no masks, shields, sanitizer

or even an ICU

within a hundred miles

your *middle class* proving harder to reach

in their Zoom meetings, concerts

a virtual pantheon:

       Blessed Google, Holy Zoom

       Saints Amazon and Fresh Direct

       Brother Apple, Father Facebook

slows me down

but others enervate themselves

live free or die

spurn their Cassandras

I'm beyond good and evil every day

jump, infect, and spread

growing data's what I do

Something Must Have Told Me To Ask

Shyla Shehan

After "Postcard from Trakl"*

Nature's most recognizable butterfly quivers with the weight of winter
pressing in slowly, one leaf at a time. Does she know

what comes next? Without question. Instinct from ancestors—
maps etched inside her DNA. The directive of direction imperative—

a perilous flight to warmth of oyamel fir trees in Mexico. Does she know
she might not survive? I have to ask. What was gained and lost

with the bargain for opposable thumbs? The need for answers,
insatiable. We dig heels in. We lack tools to map our own migration.

We wax vertically with our poetic pursuits, generational desires,
and greed for persistence beyond a mortal existence.

The closer we get to deciphering the zodiac, the faster it disappears.
Dim bulb made dumber the brighter we shine, exhausting

one life at a time naming each thing before it winks out.
I am an echo drifting back to myself drinking air that swarms the trees

outside my window, temporarily sharing shelter with Mariposa.
I shiver as the weight of winter presses in.

* "Postcard from Trakl" is a poem by John Yau, *Paris Review Issue no. 118* (Spring 1981)

In the Heat of Summer

Alana Urcia

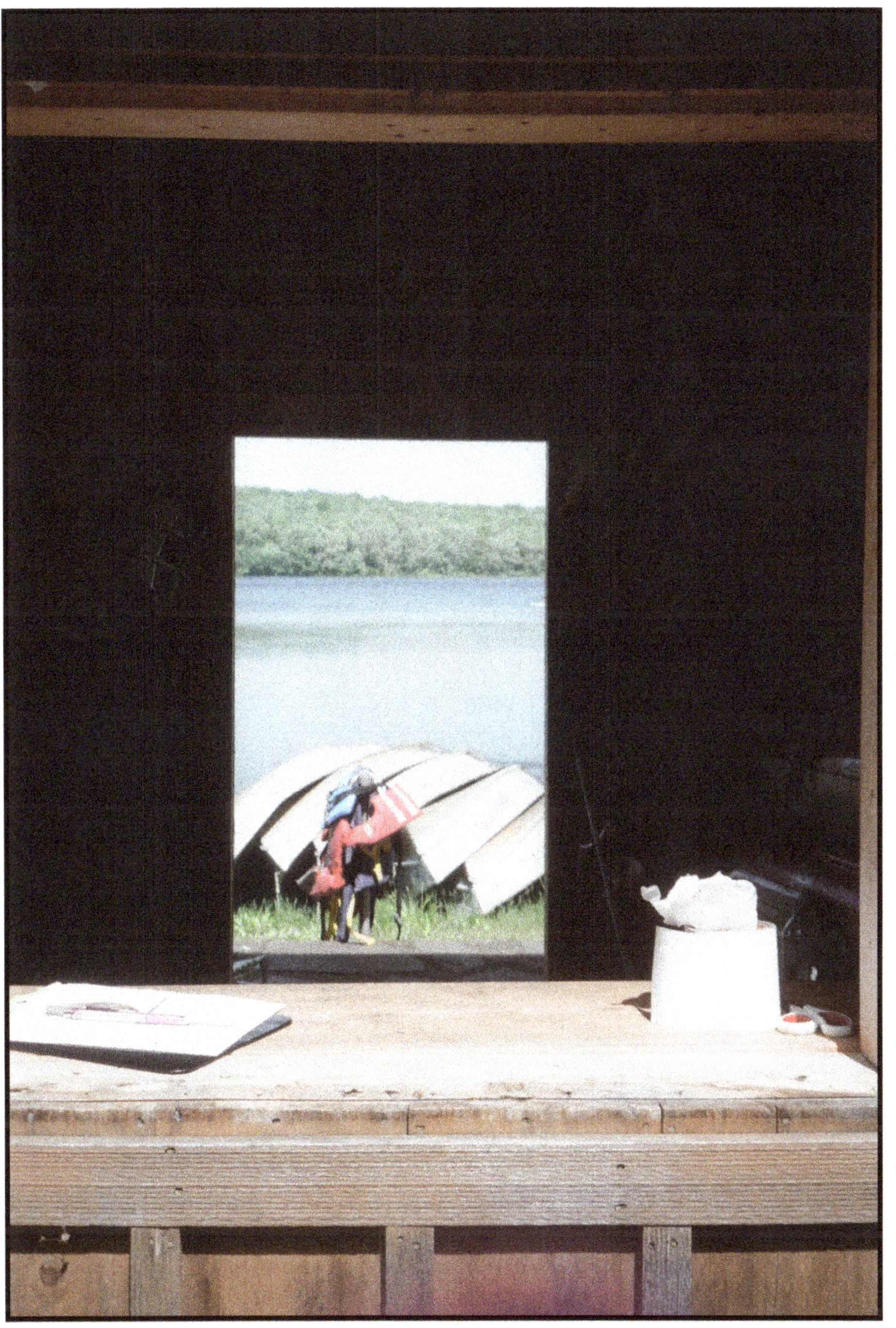

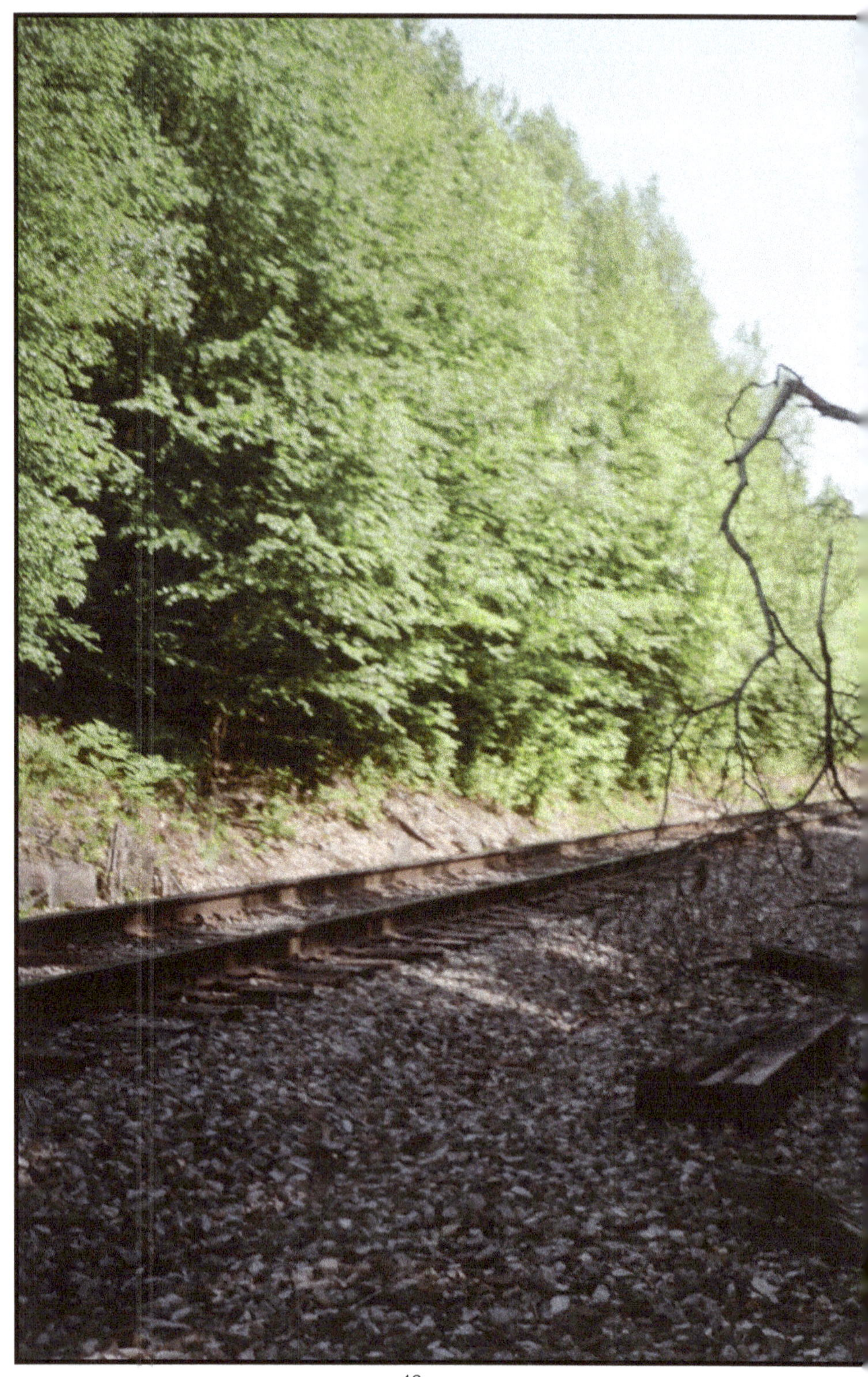

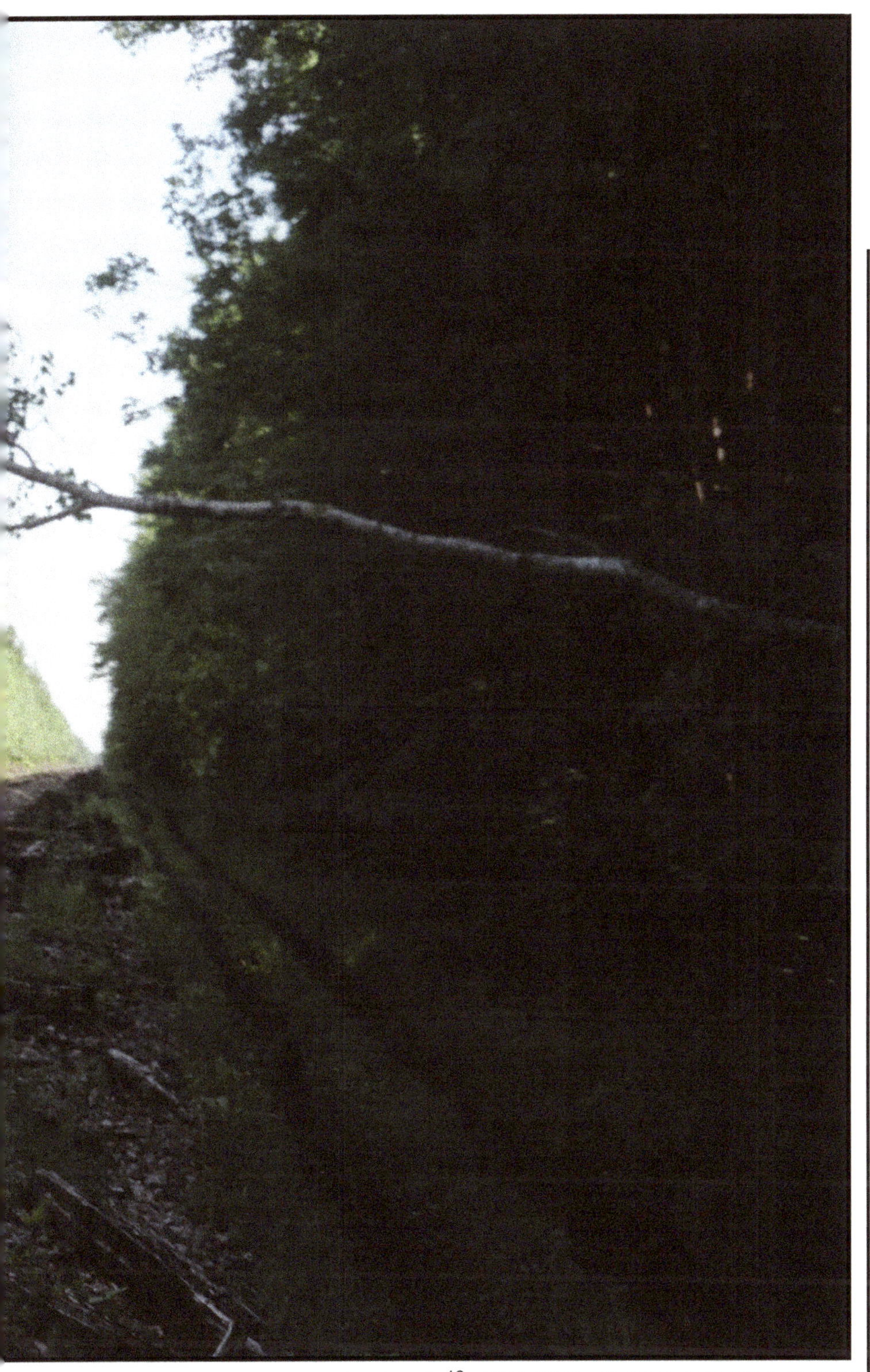

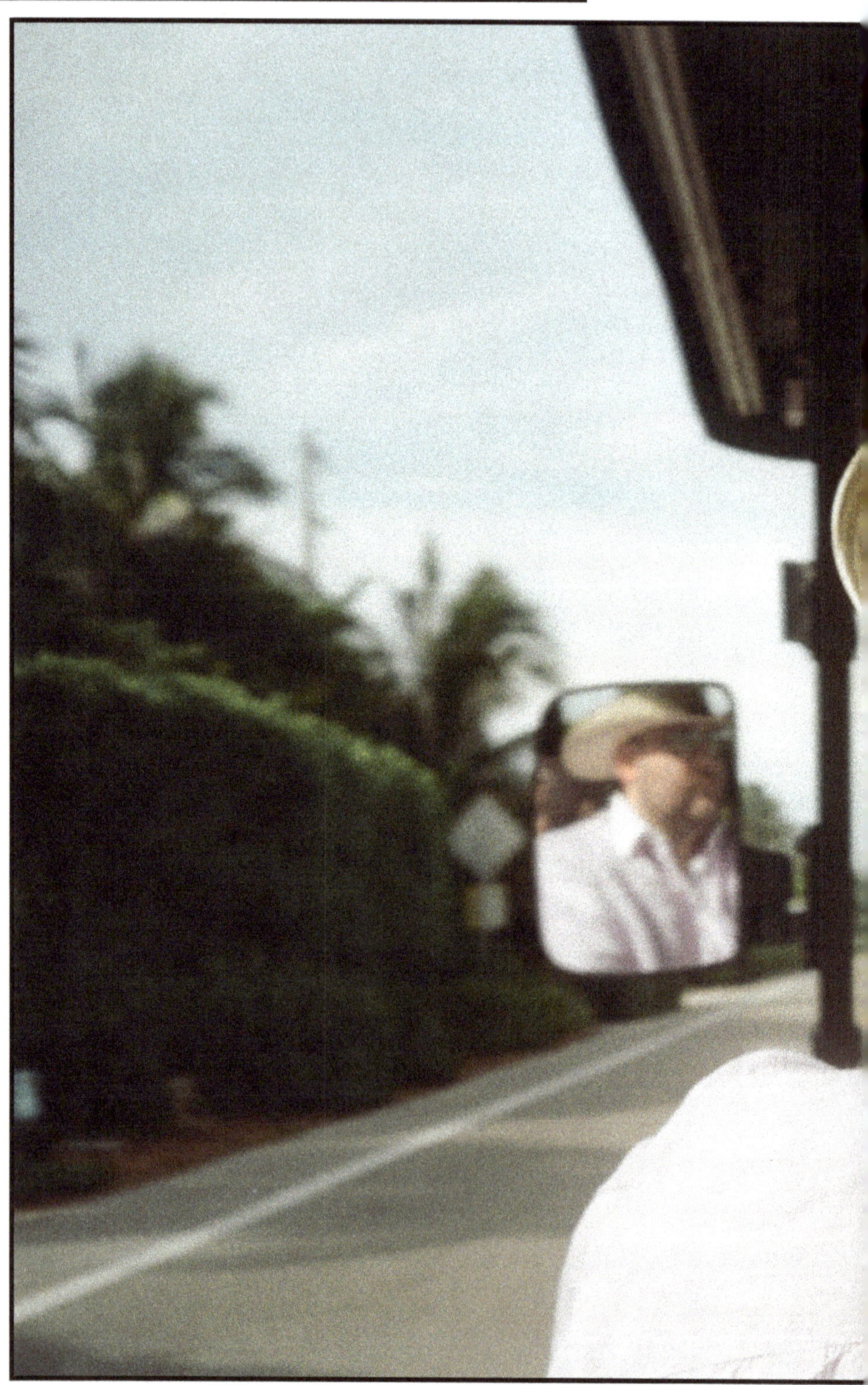

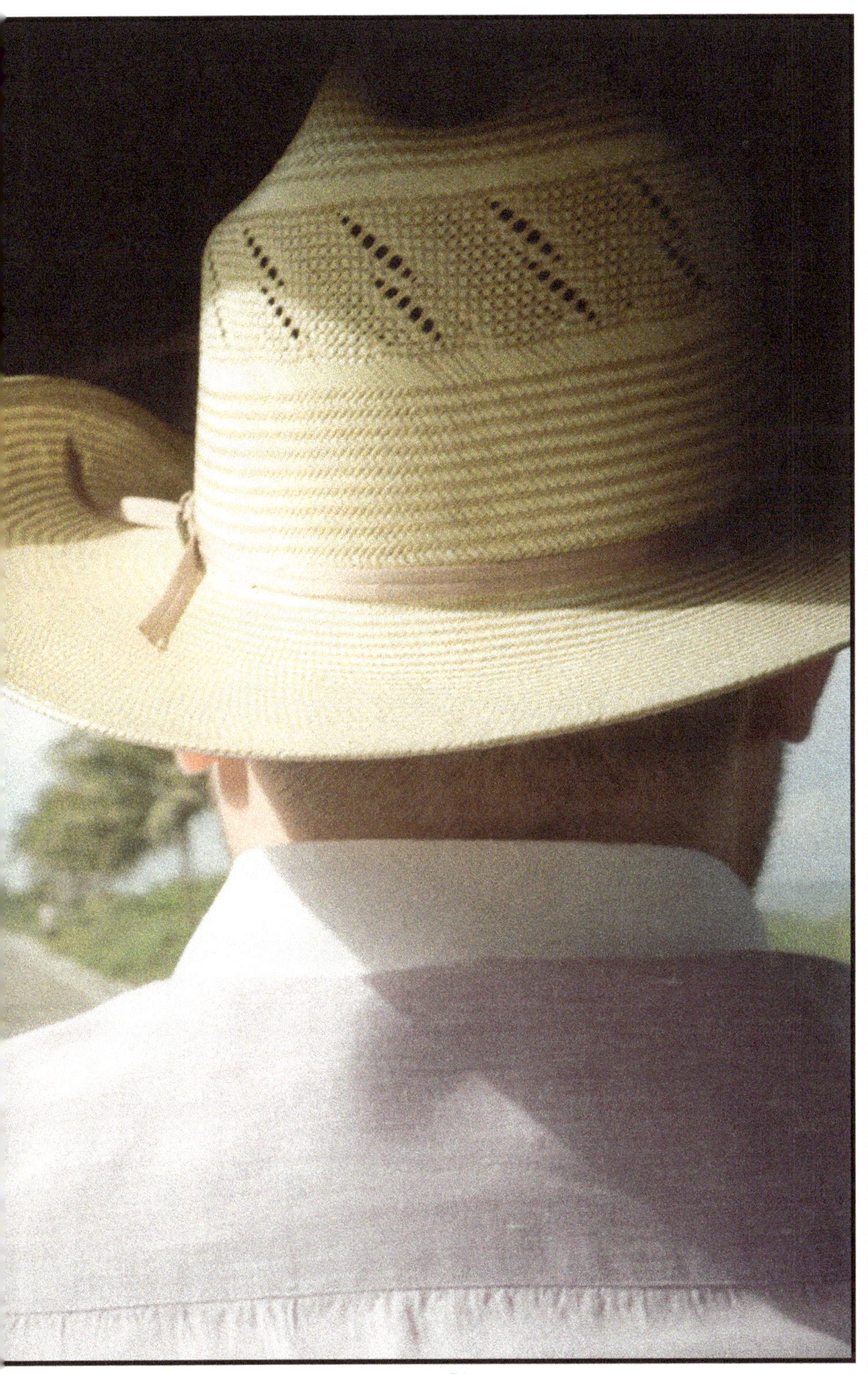

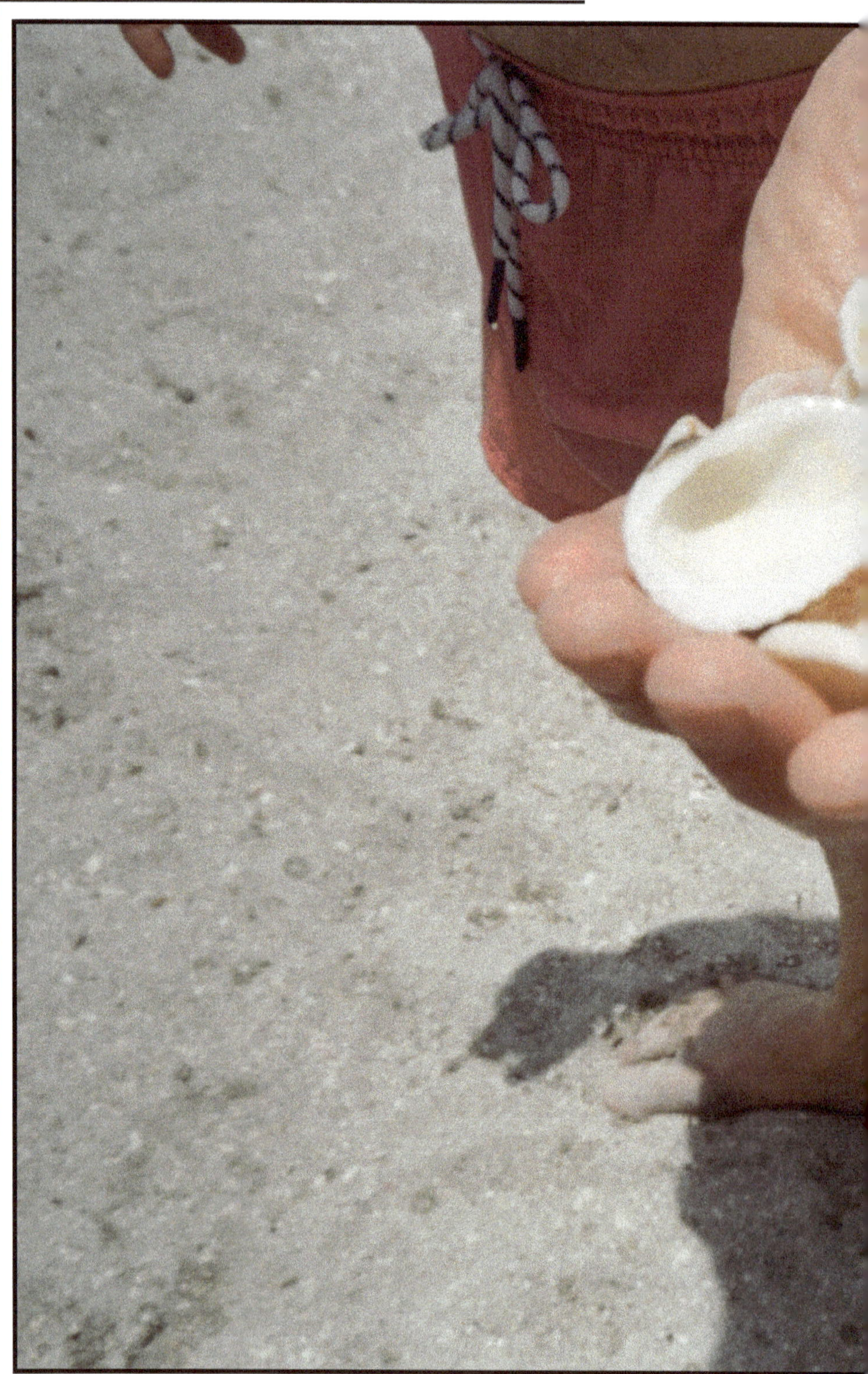

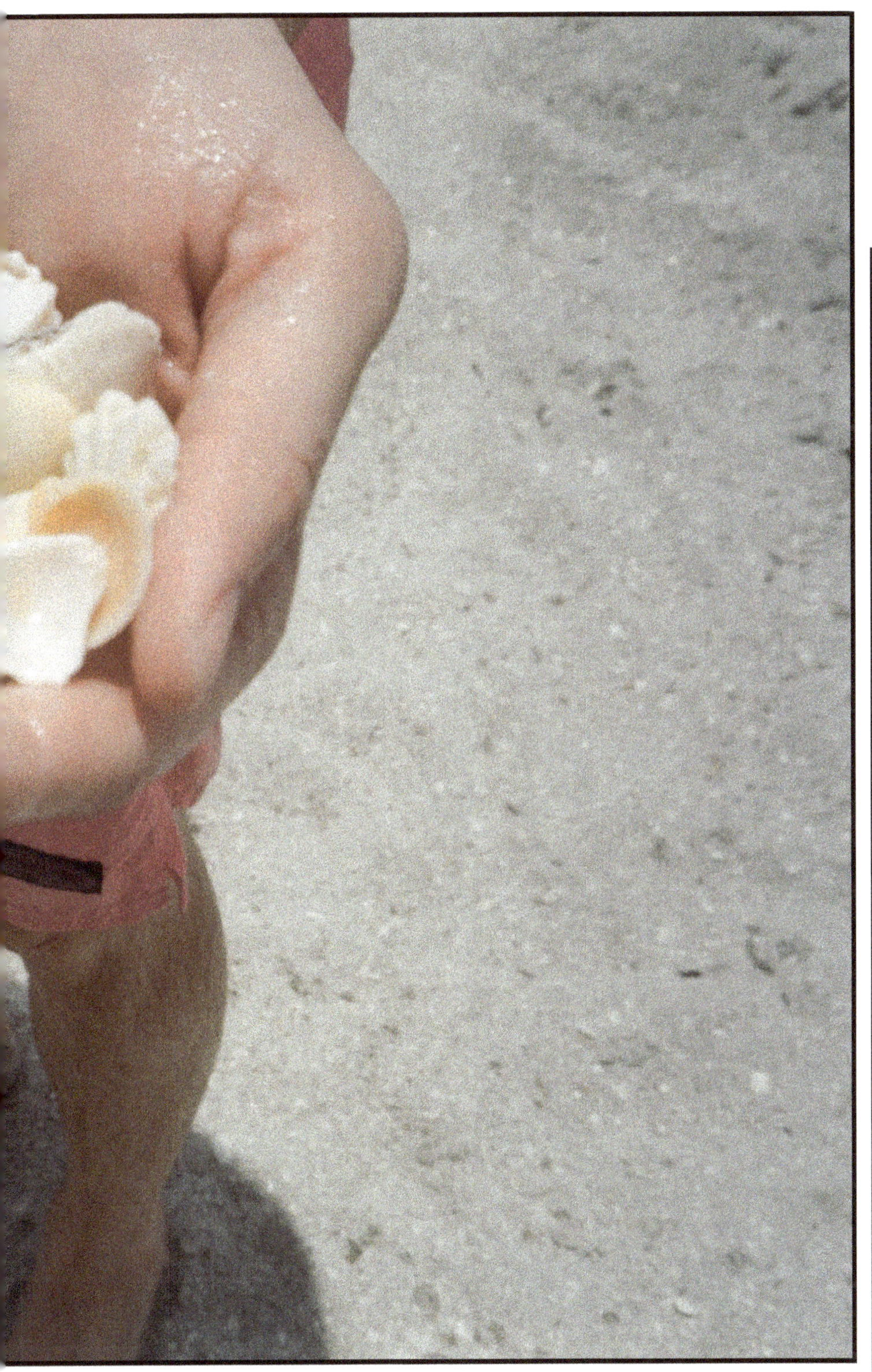

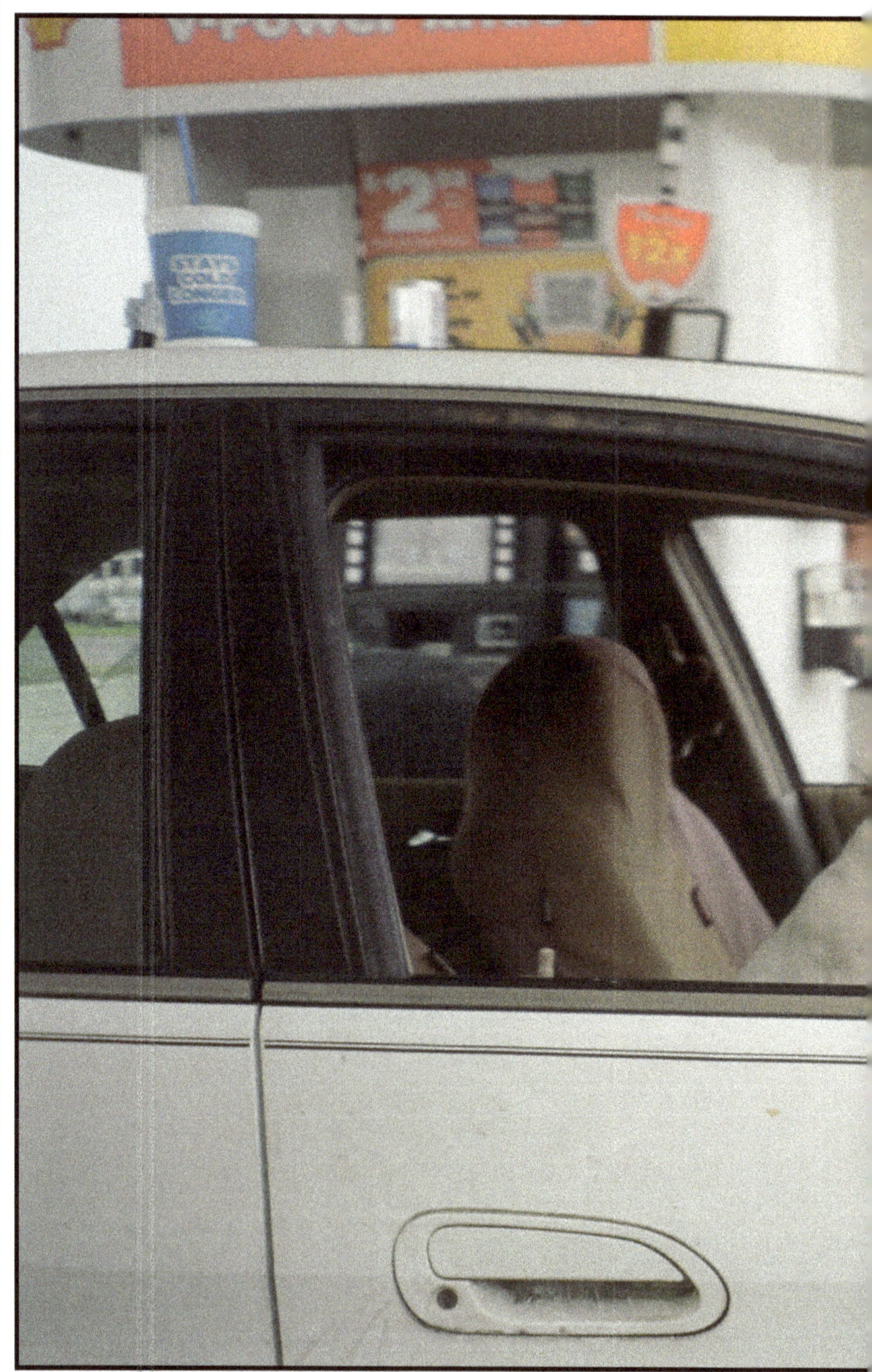

V-POWER NITRO+
$2
STATE
COLD

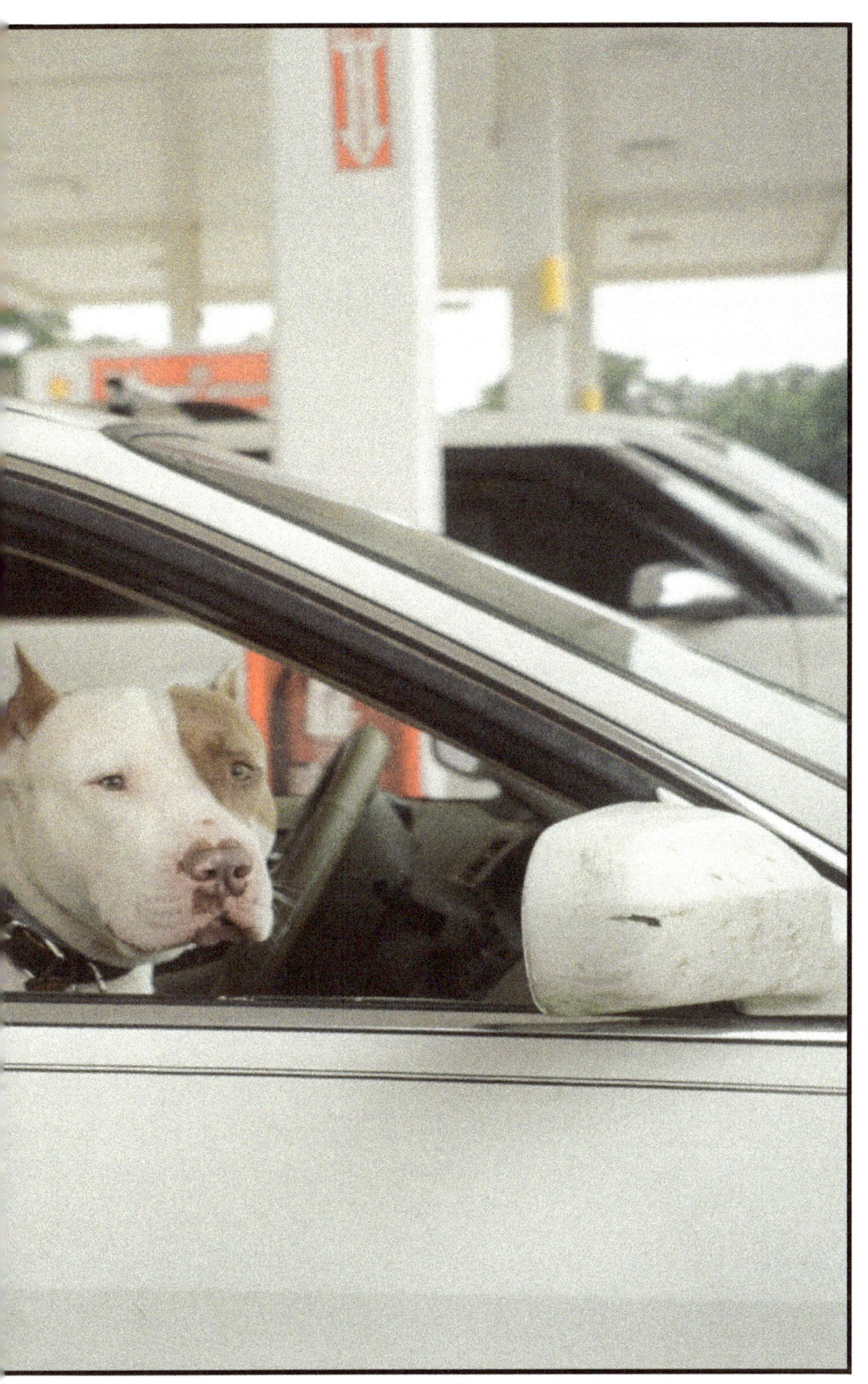

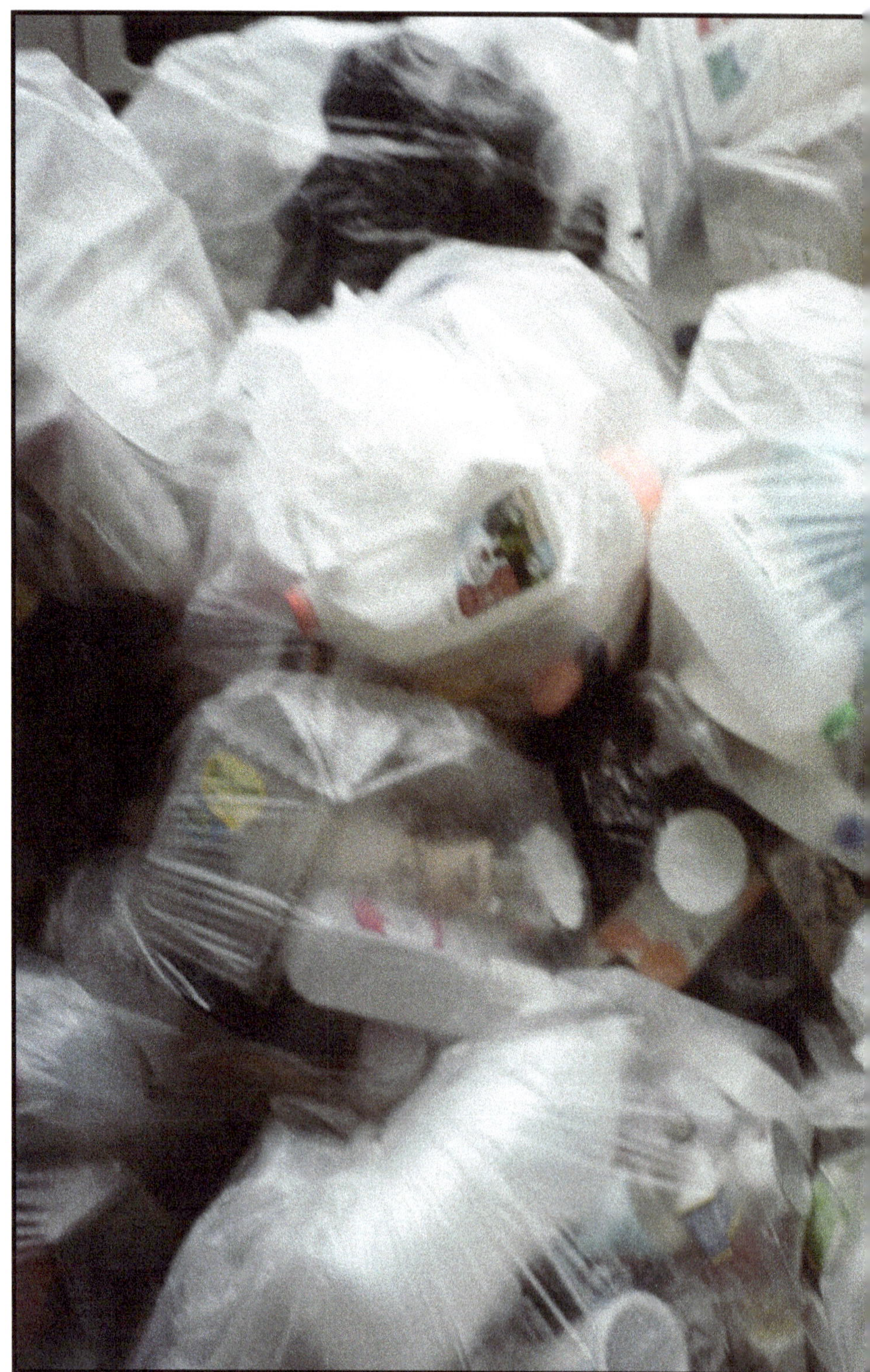

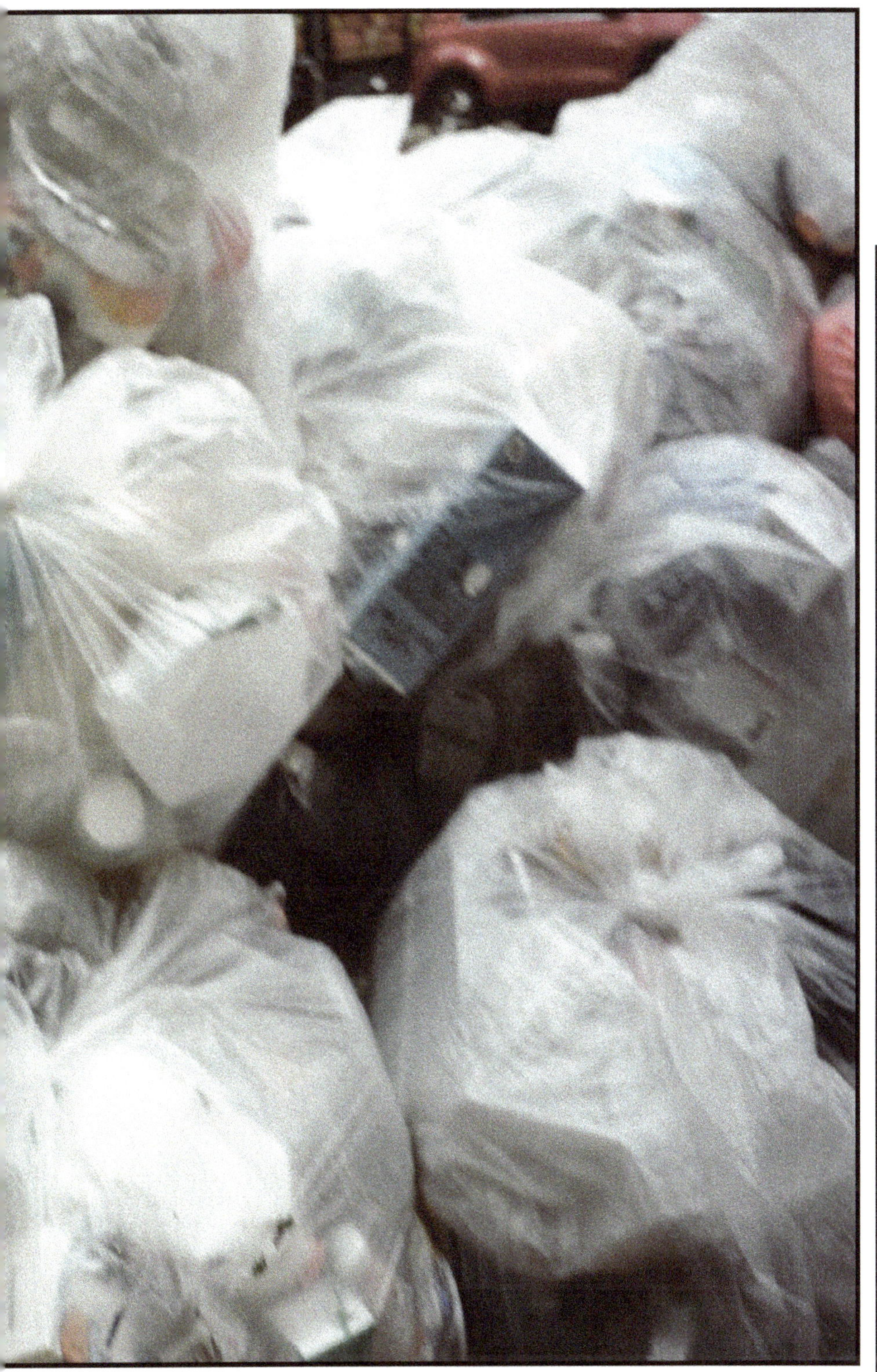

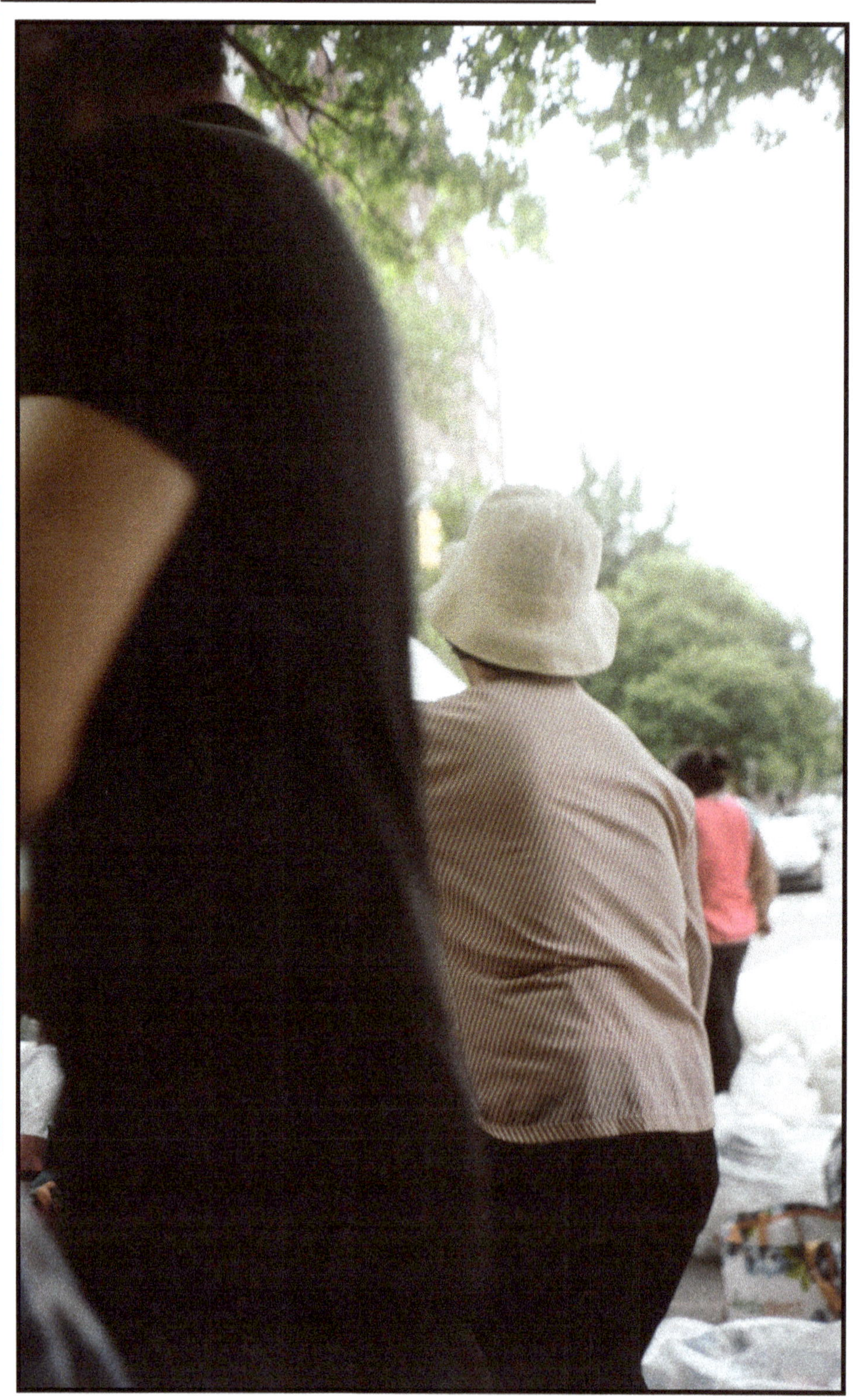

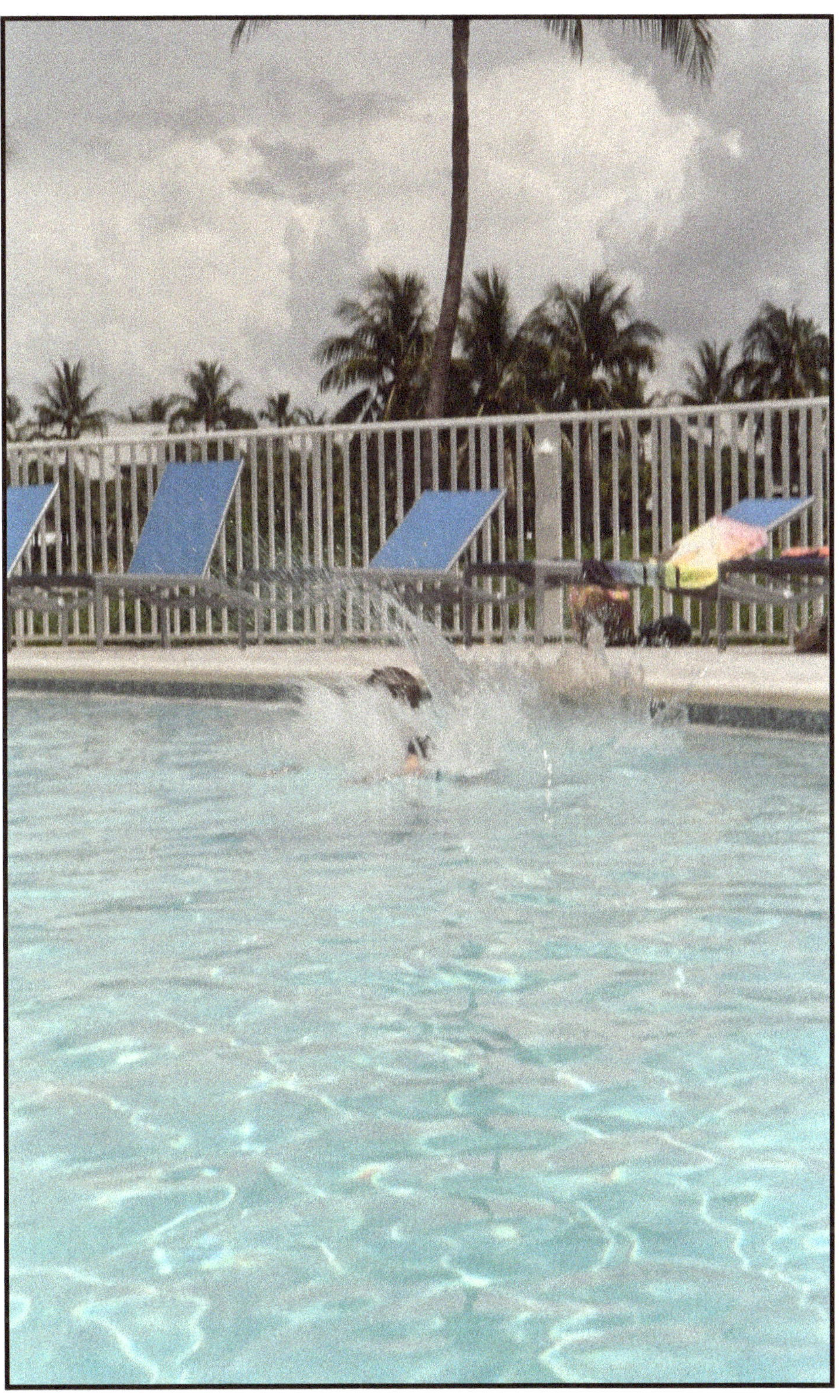

Flatlife

Chelsi Sayti

Oil rigs like
the dipping bird
toys on a desk

Milk Thistle : Shadow

Nikki Raitz

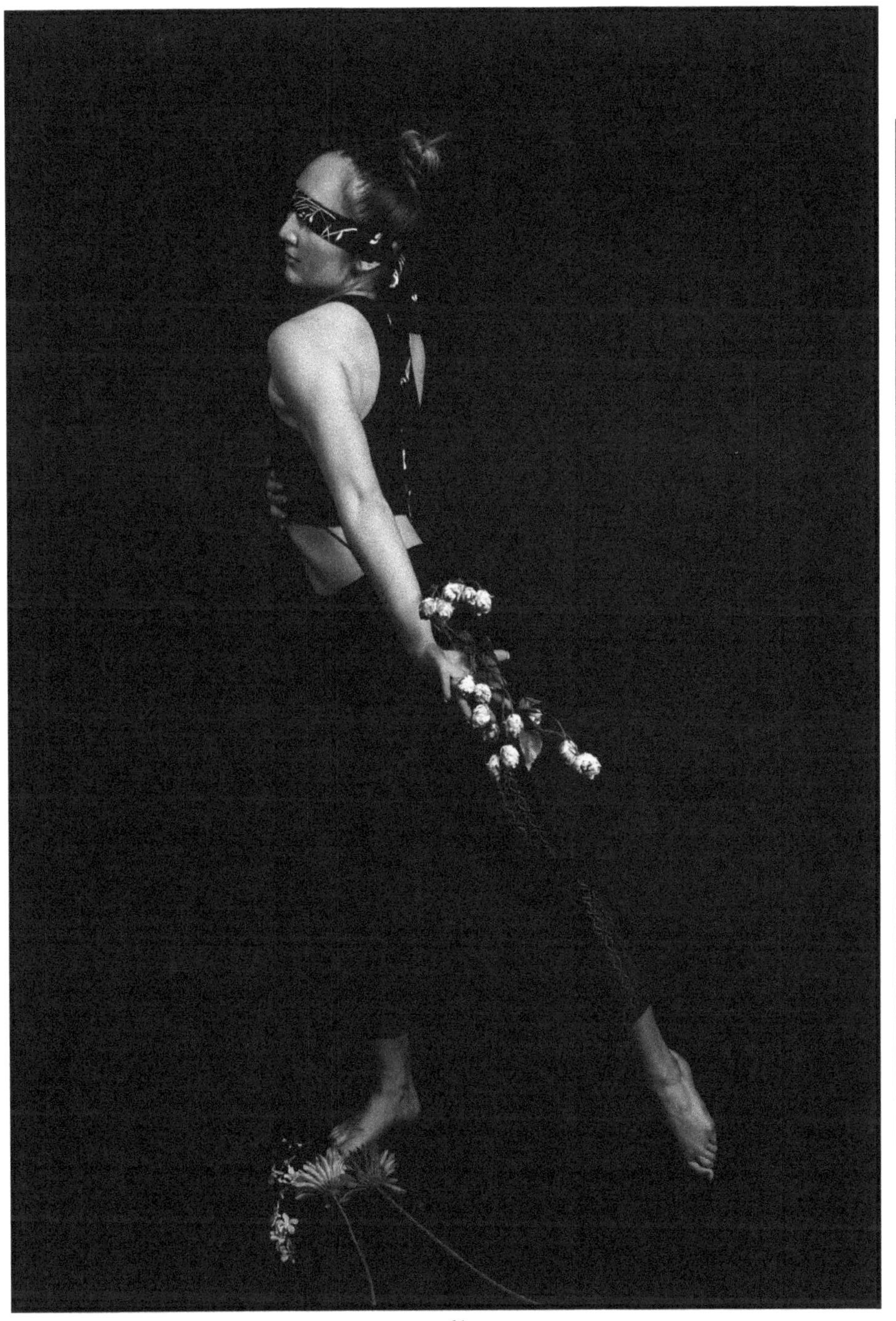

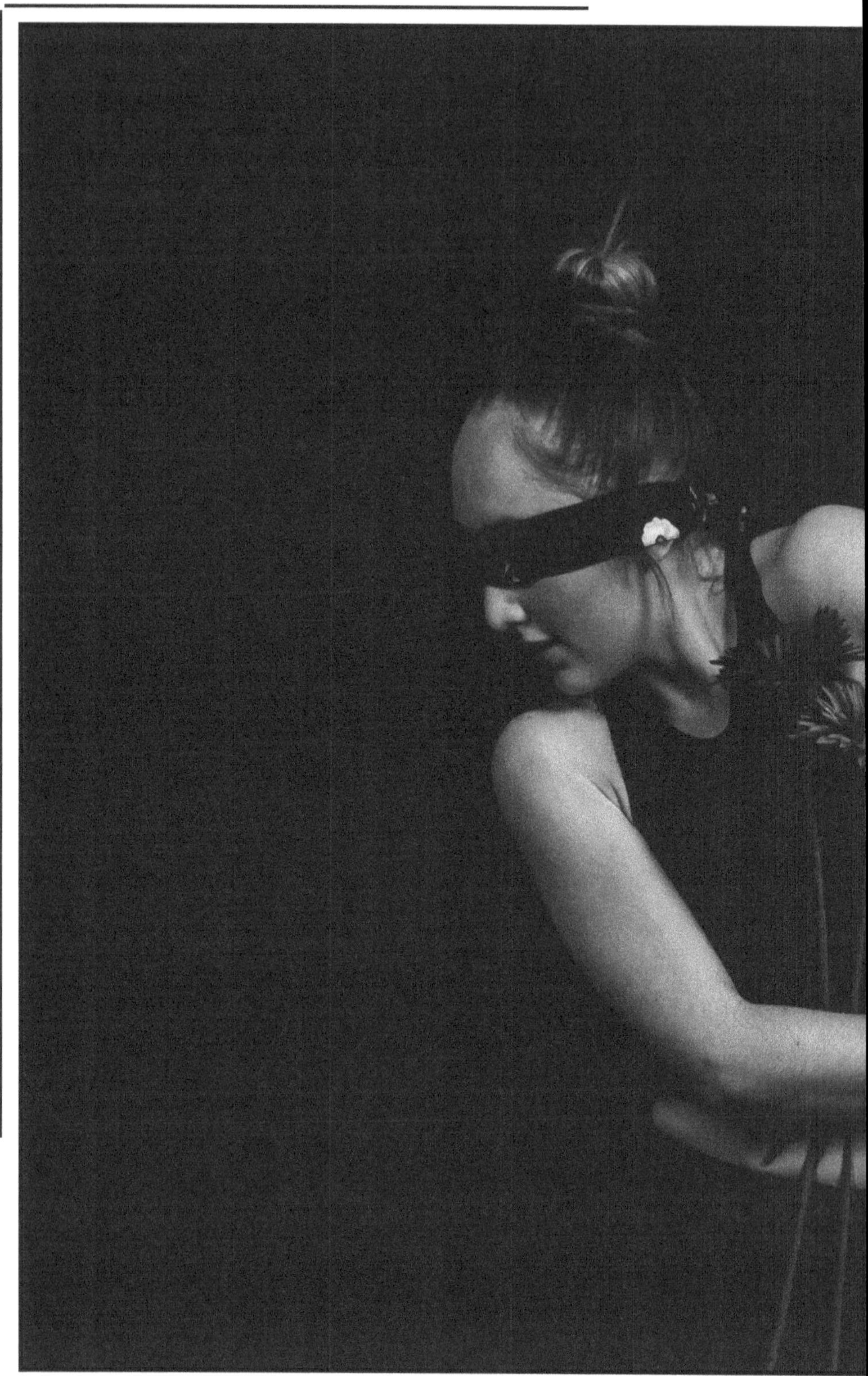

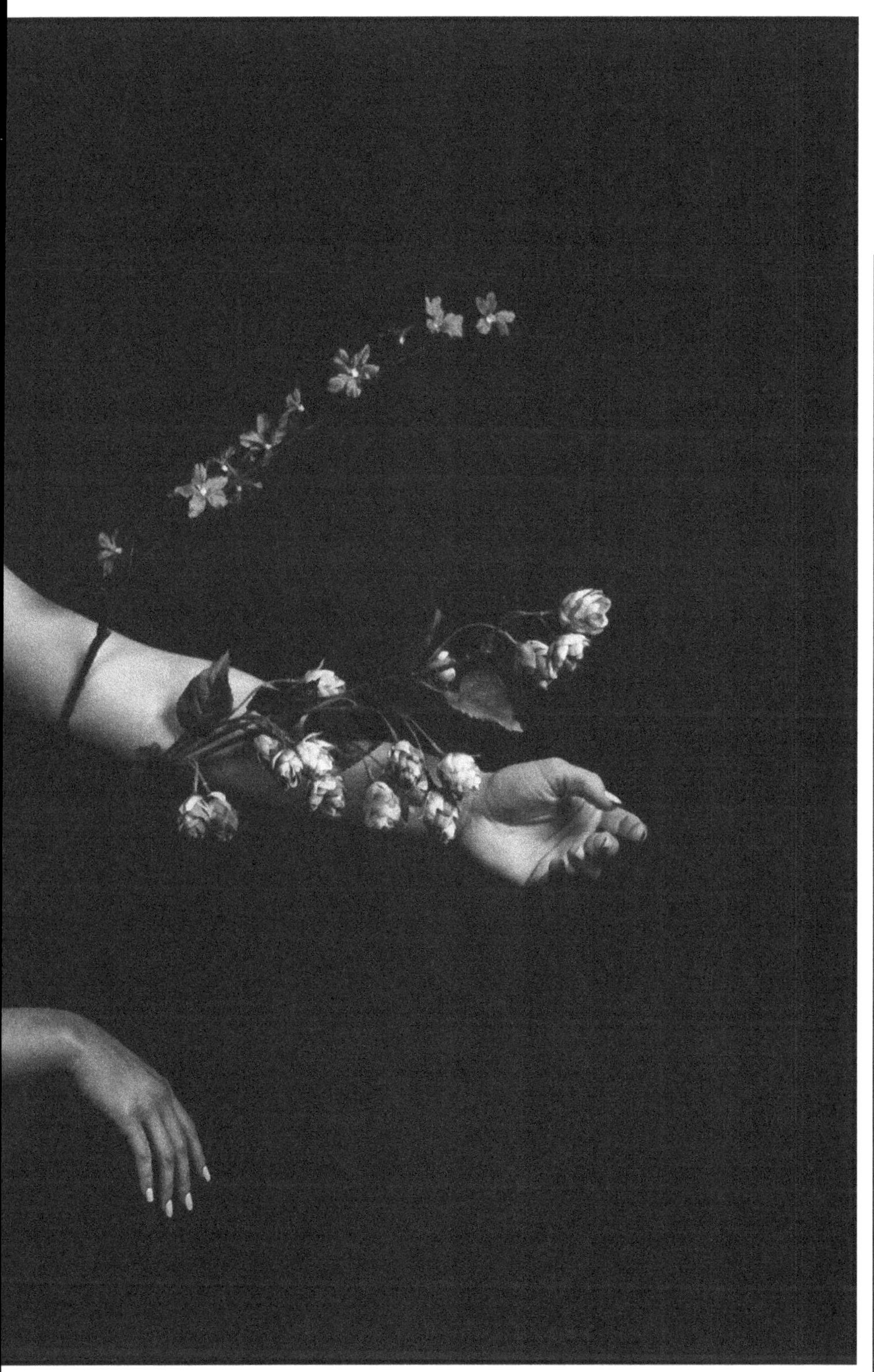

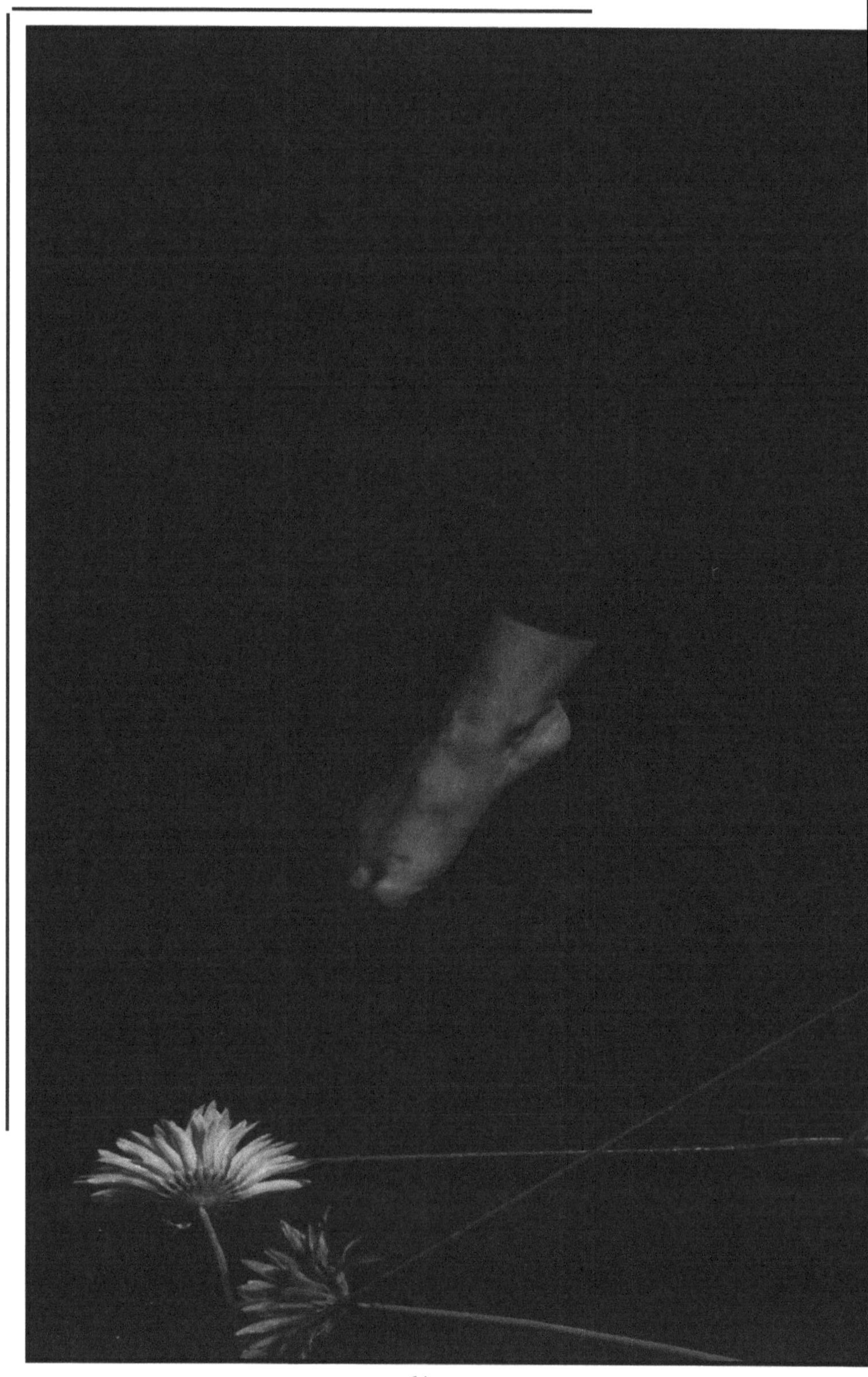

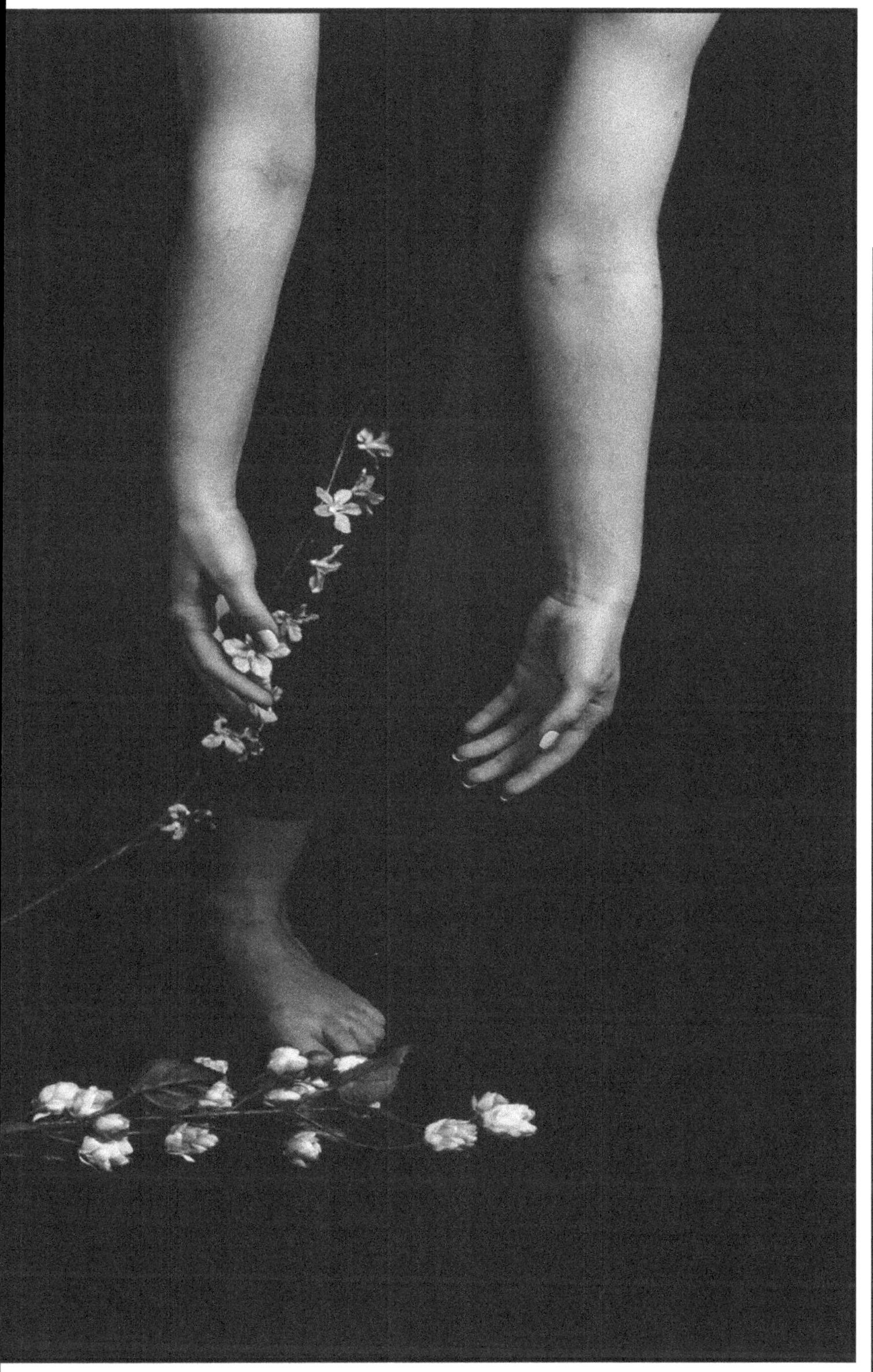

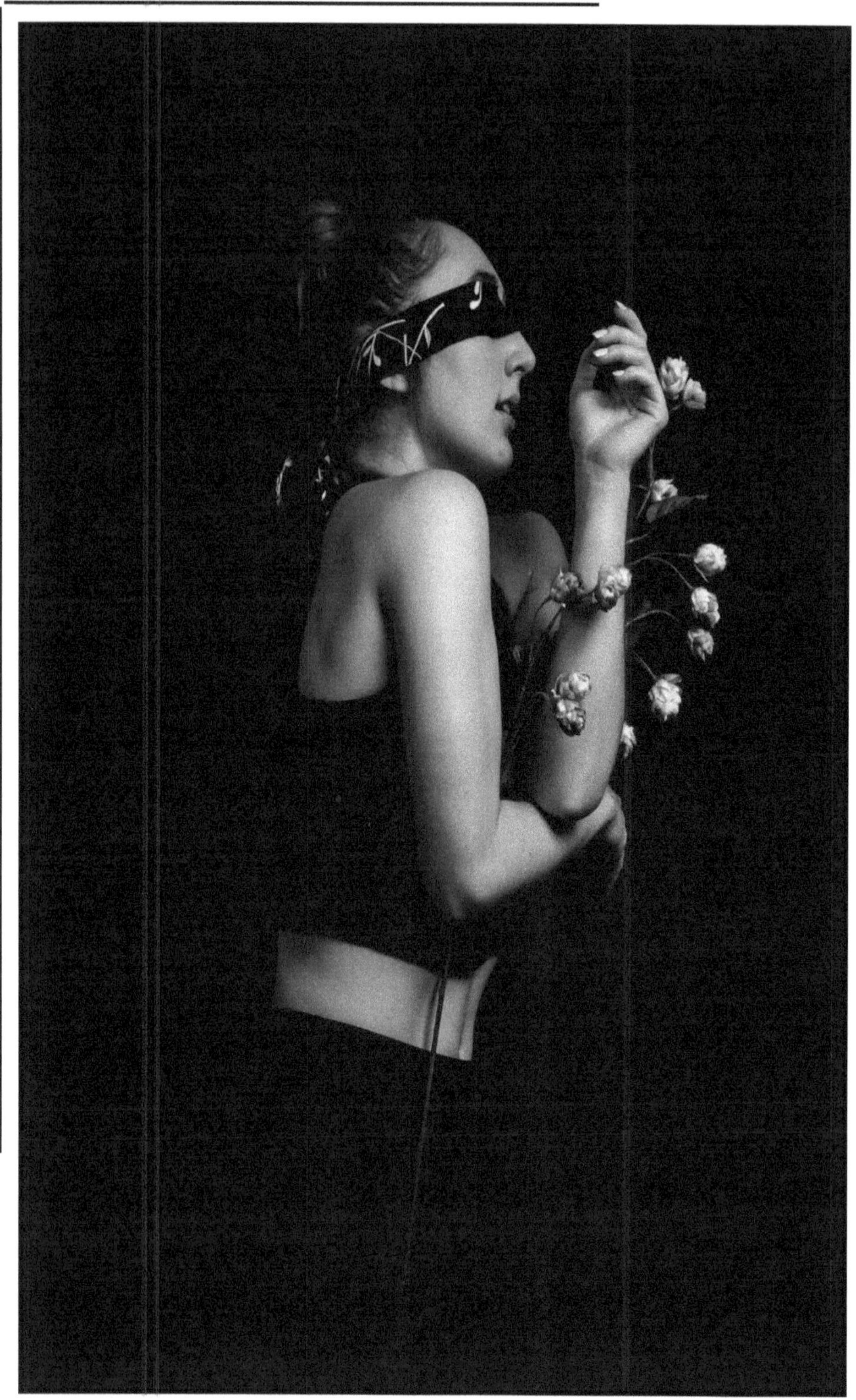

Movie Theater

Tom Skove

For the last two hours, I took it for
the better dream, and let it entertain me,

the kiss that turns stopped clocks,
relights fires, repairs what dropped.

Awkwardly, the three of us retrace our route
across the row of cushion seats.

The blued lights go back on.
Two boys come out with brooms and mops.

I feel the sword thrust into my coat pocket
dissolving. The next remark I make surprises me.

A paper tub of popcorn brandishes its remaining
pure white bits against the gum-sweet floor.

I let someone else pick it up.
My hands search out the car keys in my pocket.

The transition from the theater to the street
is full of people waiting to get in.

The woman that we watched the movie with
introduces us to her special friend.

Both praise each other in excited voices
as if we ourselves were in a film.

I take a step back to get the proper distance
to watch the scene play out.

Then the clocks stop again, the fire dies out,
the broken parts scatter across the carpet

such that you can't make out what the object was.
The two friends seem to tire.

We turn to leave, and nothing that happened
after that was worth remembering except the music.

Learning to Drive

Eric Braman

I used to mix CDs with
flavors ranging from
cayenne to vanilla.
They filled a book in
my sidekick footwell.
Sharpie etched surfaces
read a message to readers,
"Beware s/he who listens"

I never understood how
to follow heartache
with hard rock, but with
water-filled eyes I cast
a net, pulling sonnet
and virus from the dark
web. I learned to drive
by sliding cars into ditches.

I used A/C in winter cuz
it was easier than taking
off my coat. In summer
I lost sunglasses in
glove compartments
and let gummies melt
across my dashboard. My
car collected my mistakes.

I had CDs I only played
when I drove alone. I don't
remember what songs
were in the mix, but I
recall the shame of them.
Seventeen tracks for
seventeen years I
didn't like myself,

but I pretended to.
I learned to drive by
running stop signs
and T-boning fragile
elders in larger cars,

by smashing face-first
into airbags and crying
on curbsides. I hated

myself and didn't know
how to keep my eyes
on the road while
changing channels. One
time I drank bad beer
in the basement of
someone's house I
barely knew. He played

a song on my secret CD.
I drove my car into a
traffic sign and learned
I hate myself, but should
improve my driving. I was
seventeen and I pretended
with CDs in footwells and
eyes barely on the road.

I learned to drive by
plowing through snow drifts
and hitting the brakes too
hard. I just remembered
Norah Jones was on my
secret CD. I pretended I
didn't hate myself. Over
time, I got better at driving.

Parts of the Temple in Istanbul

Eva Swiecki

Mice were following you and showing up dead,
    faceless ladies wearing red coats waited on benches and
                    followed me home,
             but it didn't matter.
By this time, you've superimposed your sweet
      mystique and driven me into a manic state: lunar + wild =
a lonely, vulnerable girl approving all imperfections, even looking
       desperate: rolling around in bed in front of you pleading
            I miss you.
You are oblivious and talking about the parts of the temple in Istanbul
    I can't remember the name of that were once used to
communicate war messages
           by shouting from the top,
           but only serve decorative purposes now.
I'm always shouting in my head but people think I serve decorative purposes.
           I'm not used to a puzzle I can't figure out—
what a cunning way of condescending you have:
    make me feel cheap by constructing a space where it's effortless to project
my own insecurities into a wet handle.
      "You don't need it."   But you said that's not how you meant it.

This is just the beginning
    of the movie when you think the lead is charming,
        but you see only one or two parts of a much vaster person who
        more often than not is
worrying,   fighting,   and sometimes even   critiquing you—
    an elusive specificity of a protagonist you will eventually
        fall in love with,
          even though she's like gravel and cable television.
    Maybe you'd run if you knew better.
      I have a feeling you might,
        but something is stopping you.
        I don't really mind:
mice know their way around a maze the second time around.

If a Stop Sign Falls

Eric Walker

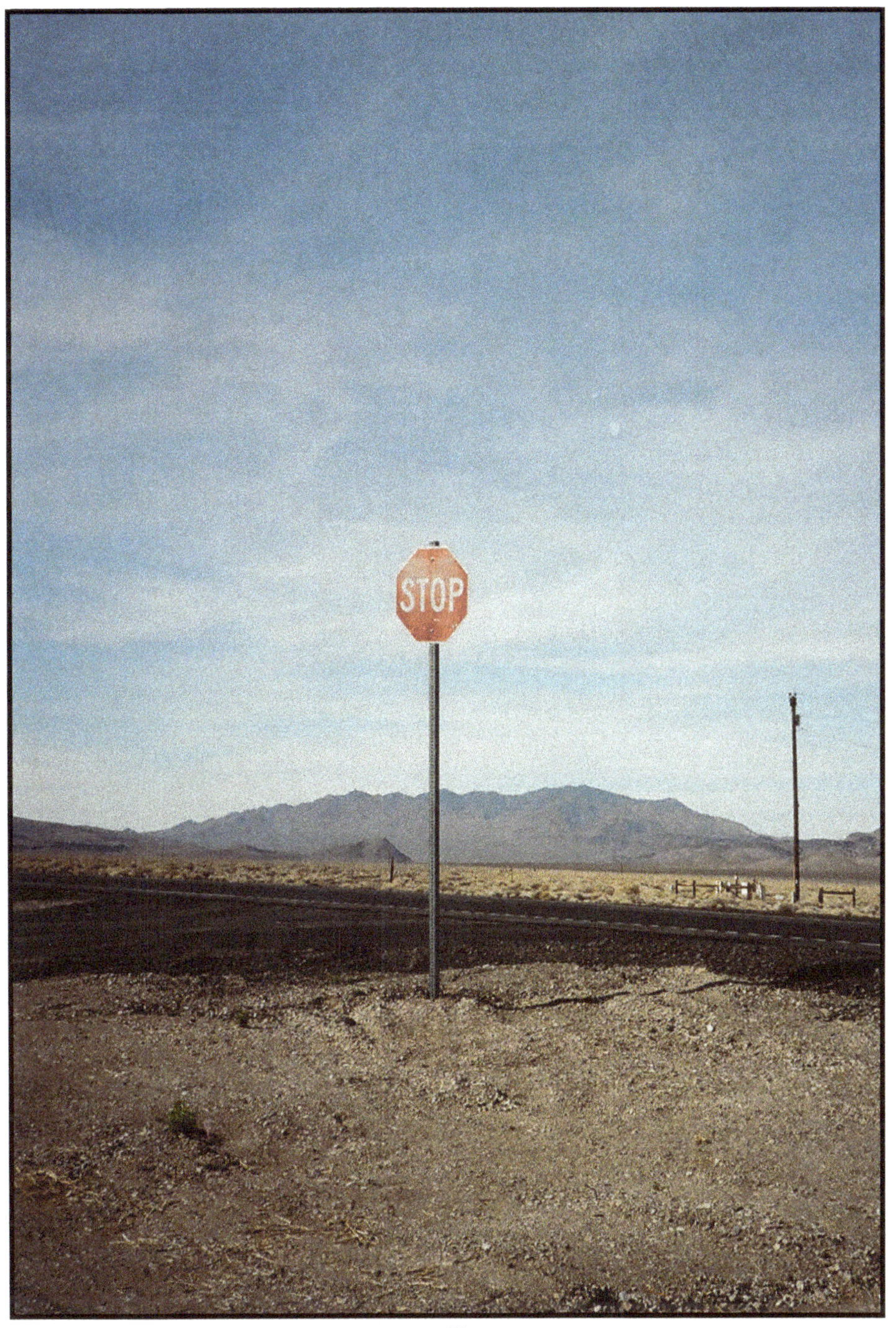

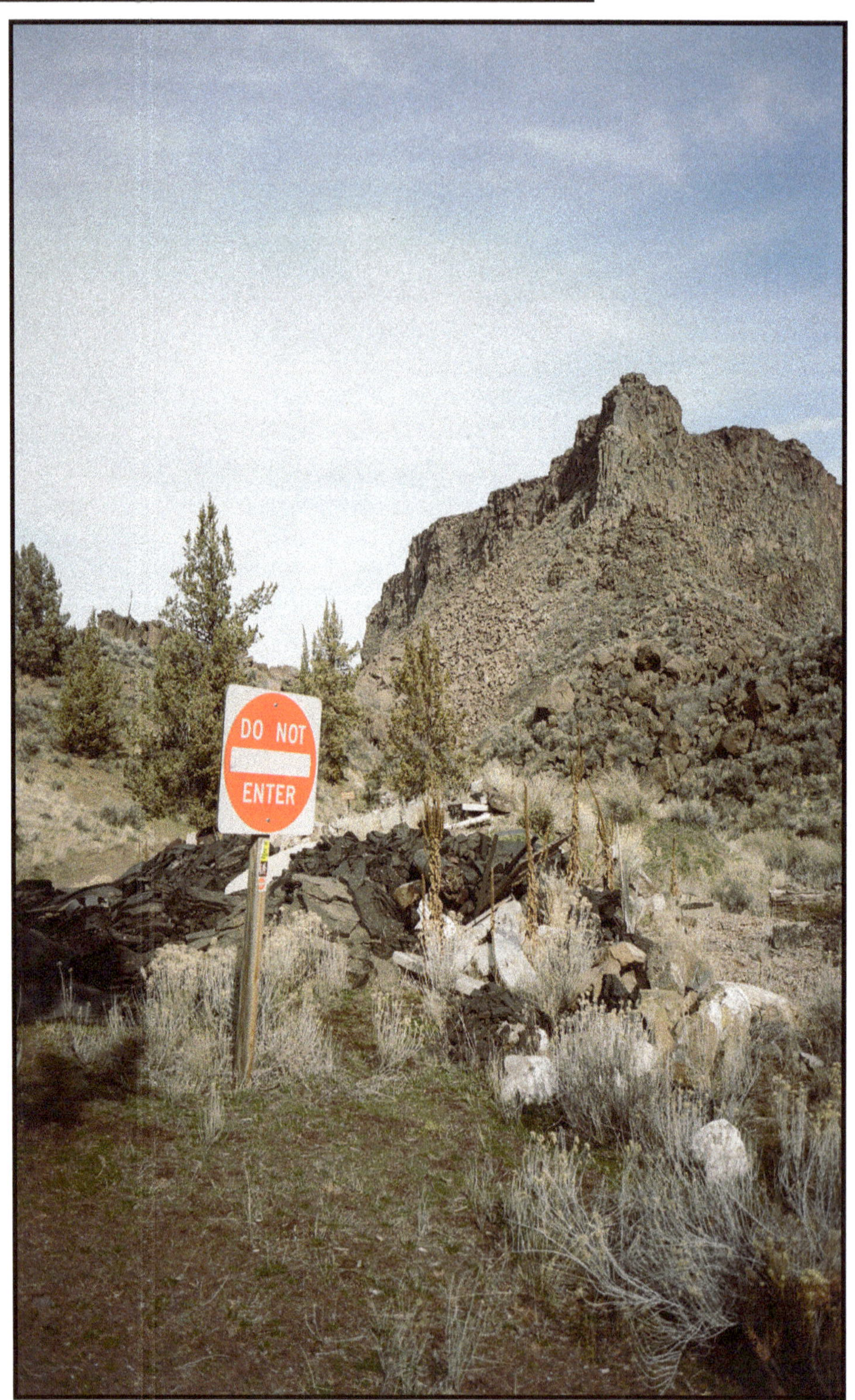
DO NOT
ENTER

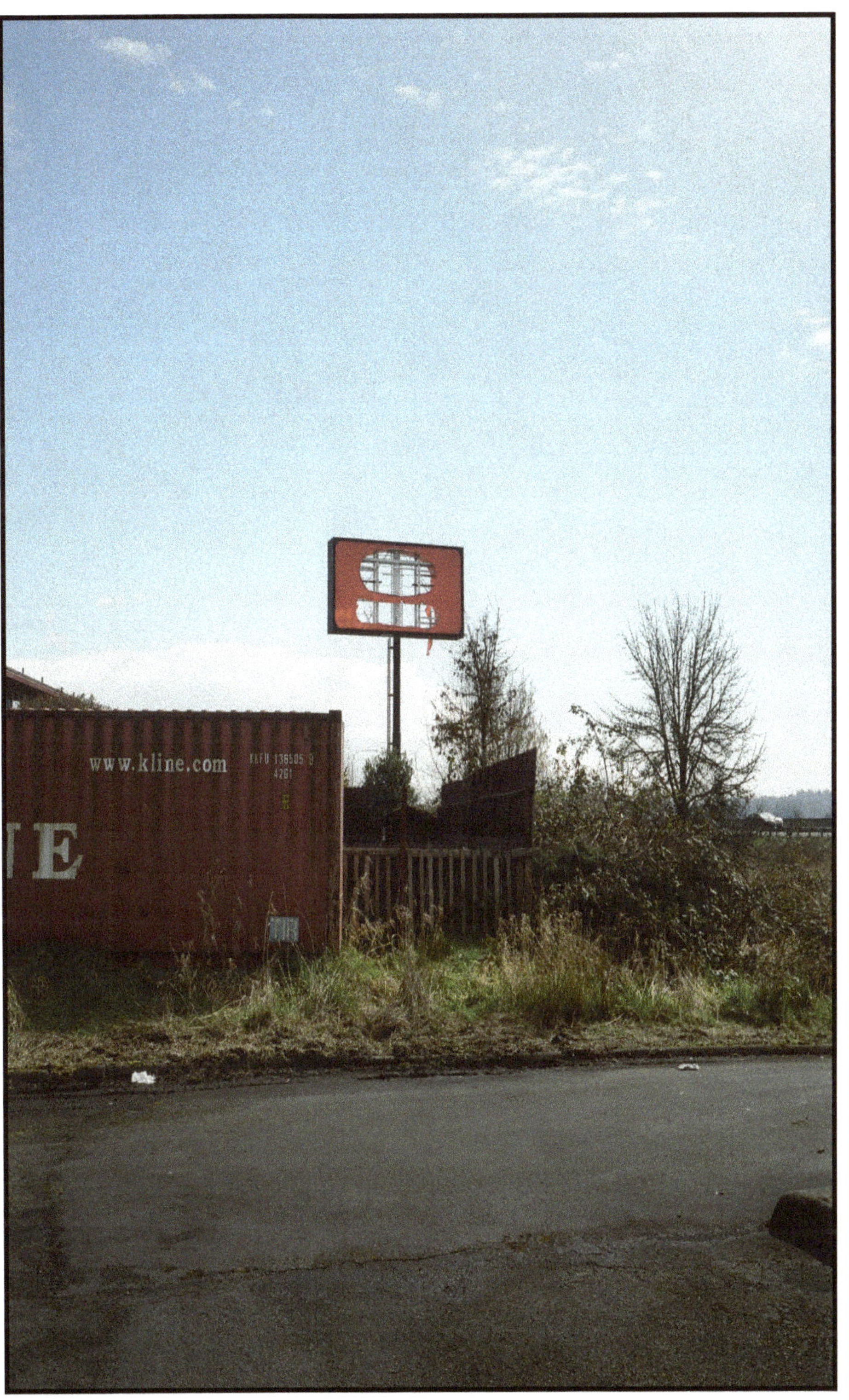

www.kline.com
KKFU 136505 9
42G1
E

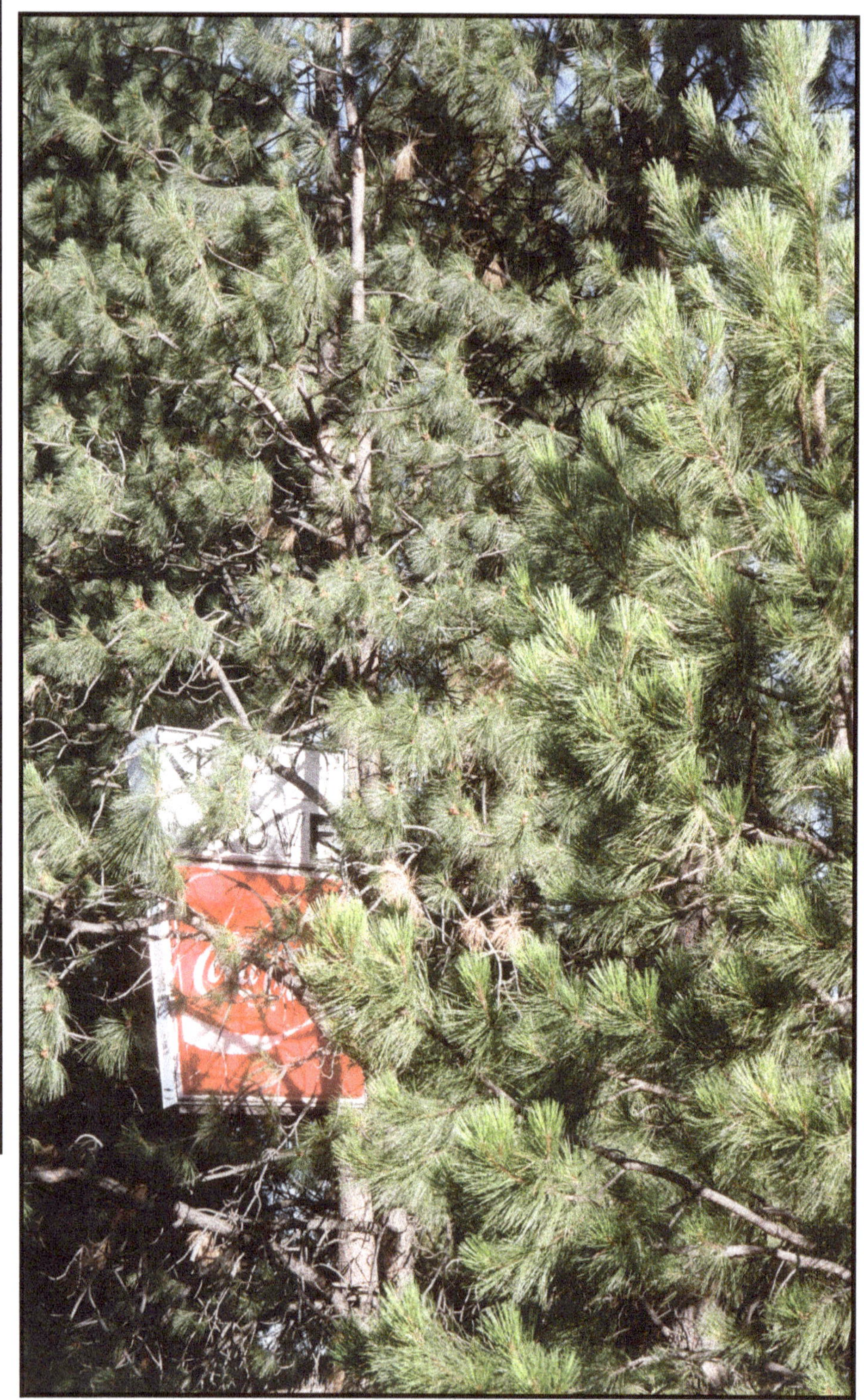
VE
Coca-Cola

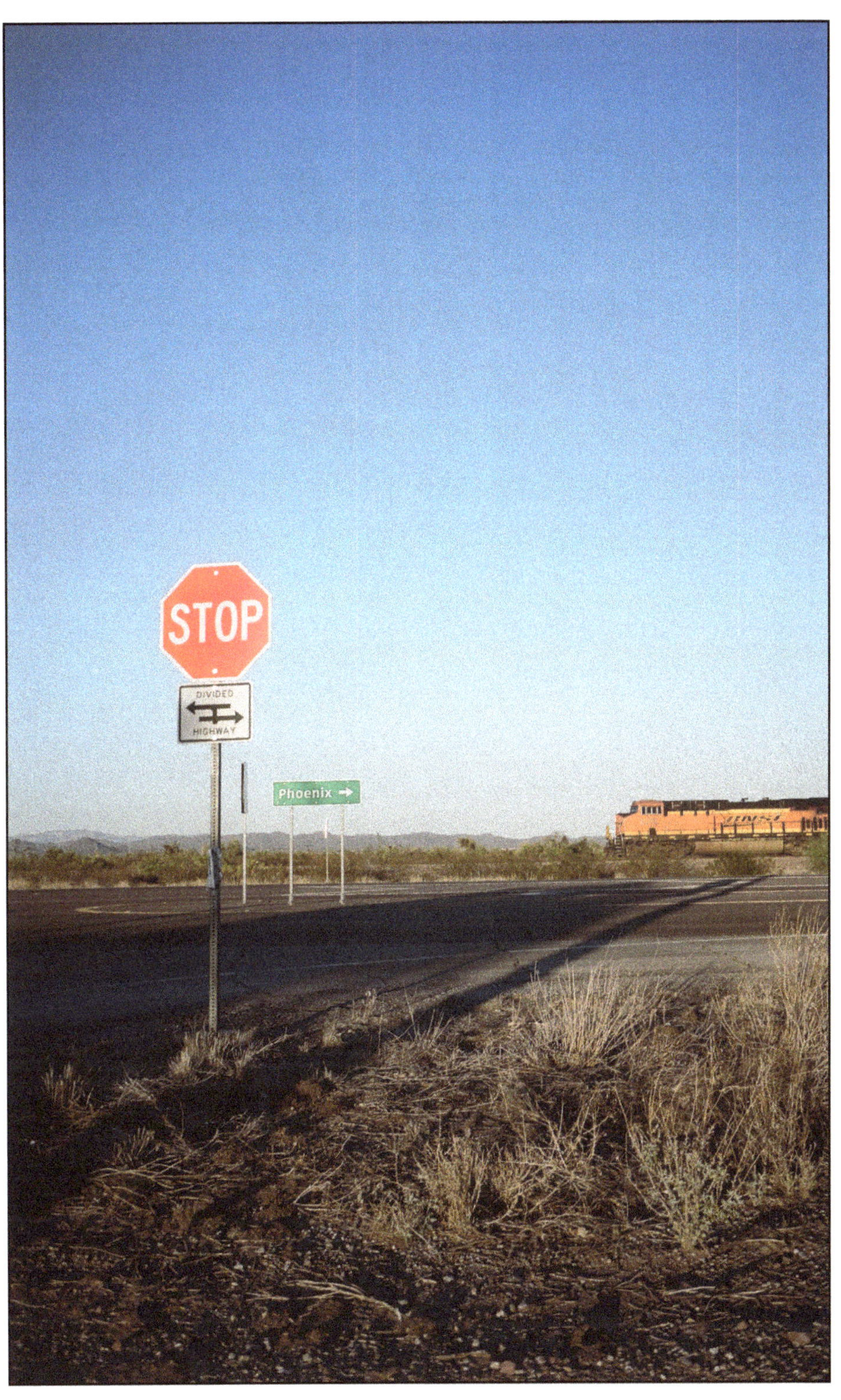
STOP
DIVIDED
HIGHWAY
Phoenix →

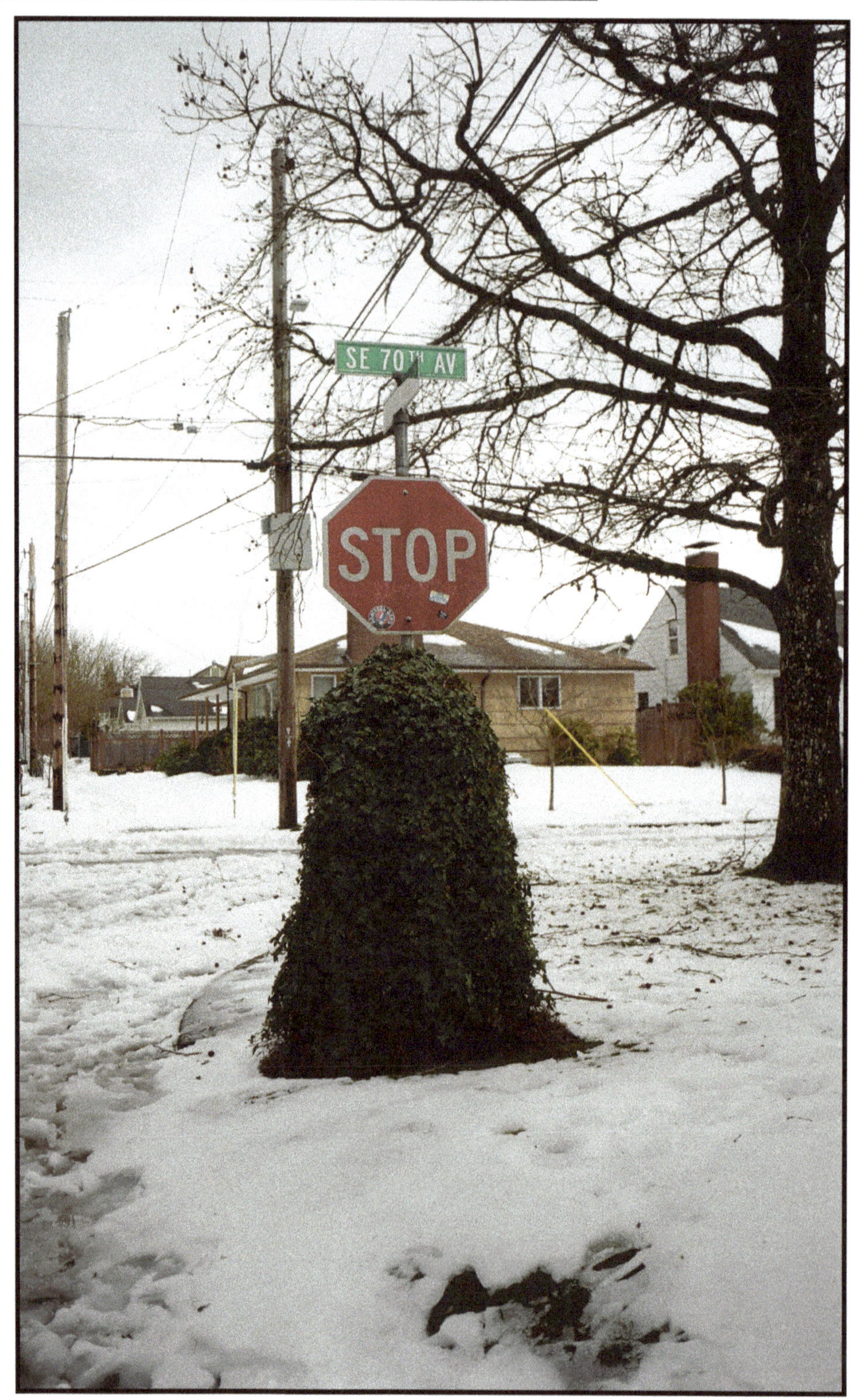

SE 70TH AV
STOP

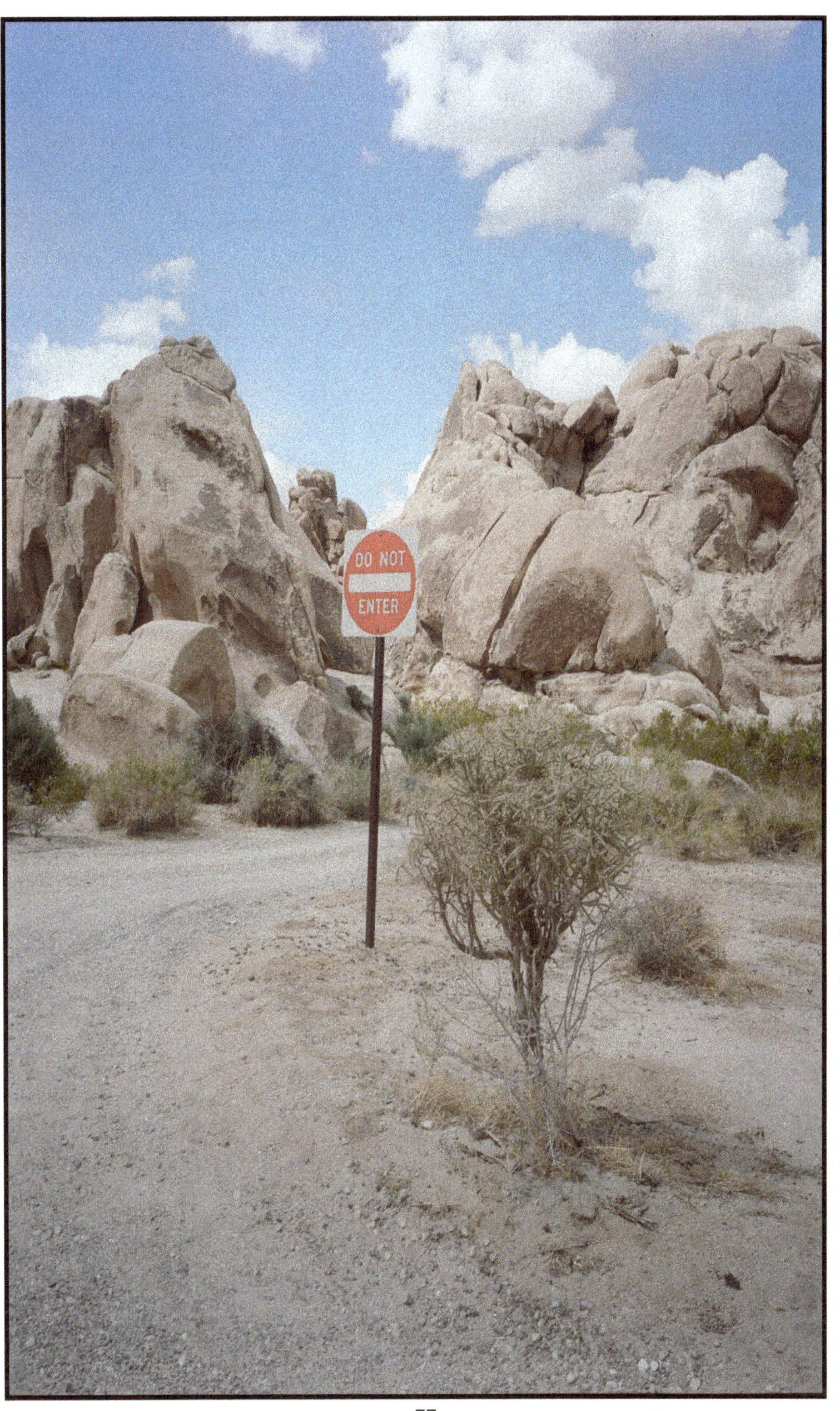
DO NOT
ENTER

Alternative Names for the "Founding Fathers"
A Campus Survey

Lara Henneman

The University Committee for Truth in History has voted that the use of the phrase "the Founding Fathers," to describe the members of the 1787 Constitutional Convention, is problematic and should be replaced in university syllabi and discourse. Student survey respondents noted that the phrase is "totally creepy" and "emblematic of the patriarchy."

Please take a moment to vote for your favorite of the following alternatives, designed to meet student demands for change while building on the positive responses that the alliteration was "pleasing" and "easy to remember." We appreciate the student body ceasing all inflammatory social media posts, particularly any TikToks featuring members of the administration in compromising positions with the group formerly known as the Founding Fathers.

American Architects
Builder Blokes
Constitutional Creators
Drunken Democrats
Electoral Enslavers
Federalist Fuhrers
Genteel Gentiles
Historical Heroes
Innovative Immigrants
Judicious Junta
Kingly Kweens
Lauded Landowners
Musing Menfolk
Nationalist Nancies
Occidental Oligarchs
Philosopher Propertarians
Quondam Questioners
Representative Republicans
Signature Sirs
Tactical Theorists
Ultra Utilitarians
Vexed Vassals
Western Wizards
Xenogenic X-men
Young Yanks
Zany Zealots

Other suggestions? Write them here. (Feel free to suggest a better X).

____

Please note that by participating in this survey you agree to waive your right to join the class-action suit for tuition reduction in the 2020–2021 school year.

The Crash of Flight AA79

Joseph Fisher

After hurtling through the tree line of Mt. Hood national forest, Flight AA79 impacted the forest floor and slid like a giant toboggan across packed snow, ice and rock. As the fuselage careened through the forest, the sounds of crumpling aluminum, bursting pressurized pipes, and the final screams of a few passengers echoed through the surrounding hillsides.

In its final resting spot amongst the Douglas-firs, the wreckage resembled a whale breaching in an ocean of snow: the fuselage laid to one side, the right-wing sticking nearly straight into the air, the other snapped in half and buried deep in the snow.

Emerging from the wreckage near the nose of the plane, a man in a pilot's uniform dragged another man by his arms. One hundred meters from the site of the crash, the men collapsed in an exhausted heap. Both men laid on their backs in the snow, breathing deeply as they looked up at the stars shimmering in the inky-black sky above.

"Thanks for pulling me out," said the man who had been dragged by his arms, his leg splayed out uselessly in front of him with each knee cap pointing in opposite directions. "I'm Mike Moore. I'm a Platinum Pro frequent flyer."

"Ah, that's great, we appreciate you flying with us Mike," said the man in the captain's uniform, still catching his breath, "I'm..."

"John Knox, and I am your captain this evening!" Both men said in tandem, prompting a bit of laughter and a jovial handshake between them.

The men laid in the snow, catching their breath and assessing their injuries, until the *woosh* of the plane's emergency door sliding open caused both men to lock their gaze in the direction of the wreckage.

"Who's there?" called out Captain Knox.

From where they sat, they watched as what looked like a large piece of luggage stood in the open emergency door before tumbling to the forest floor below.

A moment later, the luggage popped up out of the snow. Mike Moore and Captain Knox began waving their hands and calling out in the direction of the wreckage.

"Samsonite!?"

"Tumi!?"

"Kenneth Cole?"

"My name is Karen!" the piece of luggage called back. The piece of luggage turned out not to be luggage at all, but instead Karen Davenport, a burly mother of two from Bend, Oregon. Karen trudged through the snow towards the other two survivors.

"Hi, I'm Mike Moore. I'm a Platinum Pro frequent flyer," said Mike Moore, extending an arm towards Karen as she approached.

"Looks like you'll get to board even earlier on your next flight," said Karen, looking down at Mike's mangled legs.

"And I'm John Knox, I am, was, the captain of the flight," he said, extending his hand to Karen.

"Nice work Captain," said Karen as she shook Captain Knox's hand.

The three peered back at the plane, mesmerized by the ordeal they had survived. As they did, a gentle glow appeared near the back of the plane.

As the light got closer, a woman in her early 20s emerged from the darkness. She held her glowing iPhone above her head in one hand as she struggled to walk through the waist-deep snow towards the group of other survivors.

"We have to eat someone!" the young girl yelled out towards the group.

"What'd she say?" asked Karen, turning to Captain Knox and Mike Moore.

"We have to..!" the girl started yelling again before sinking back into the snow, unable to finish her thought as she tried to wiggle free of the snow's grasp.

"We have to what?" Captain Knox asked, looking at Mike Moore and Karen.

"I don't know, I can't hear her," replied Mike Moore, cupping his hands around his mouth.

"WE. CAN'T. HEAR. YOU!" yelled Mike Moore.

"One sec!" the girl called back as she struggled to free herself from the snow's grasp before trudging towards the group.

After several minutes of struggling, the frail girl stood with the others, gasping for breath as she spoke.

"We have to eat someone," she said, extending one hand towards the group to shake while the other busily poked at the screen of her iPhone.

"Already?" said Knox, first looking at his watch before glancing at Mike Moore and Karen, "We crashed less than 30 minutes ago."

"Wait? No. Do you understand that, like, this could go really viral?" said Asheliegh.

"I agree with Captain Knox, it seems a bit early," piped in Mike Moore, "how long did the Donner Party wait?"

"At least two weeks," said Karen.

"What about the rugby team from Uruguay? How long did they wait?" asked Mike Moore.

"At least a week and that was in the Andes. Way more remote than this," said Knox.

"How many views do you think we are talking about?" asked Karen.

"I think billions, right?" said Mike Moore, "I mean, a plane crash is a lot already, but if we eat someone then that probably doubles it at least."

"This isn't just about views, people," said Asheliegh, "We are talking about going viral. Like sitting on the couch with Fallon, Colbert, and Ellen viral."

"...Maybe not Ellen," interjected Mike Moore.

"Whatever!" said Asheliegh, "drinking wine with Kathy and Hoda, eating brunch with Oprah, A FREAKING NETFLIX DOCUSERIES. This is, like, the biggest thing to happen to me, like, ever."

For a moment, the four stood in silence, each imagining their lives of fame.

"Can we eat one of the already dead ones?" asked Mike Moore pointing towards the plane, "is that ethical?"

"No. Absolutely not," said Karen, "I promised my daughter I would start eating free-range, cage-free meat or whatever."

"Okay," started Knox, "so it's one of us. How do we choose who we eat?" asked

Captain Knox.

"I don't know," said Asheliegh, "but, like, we need to hurry before someone comes to rescue us."

Each of the four looked at the others, imagining reasons why someone other than themselves should be eaten.

"Your legs don't even work, why don't we eat you?" said Asheliegh, breaking the silence and pointing at Mike Moore"

"That's so messed up to say that! I'm disabled, that doesn't make my life worth less than any of yours. And plus, how can you even consider eating a Platinum Pro Frequent Flyer?" cried Mike Moore.

"You aren't disabled," said Knox, "you're injured. They aren't the same thing."

"Yeah, and a lot of good those frequent flyer miles are now," said Karen.

"No," Mike Moore said, "but having Platinum Pro status means I'm all fueled up on complimentary snacks and beverages from the airport lounge so I'm way more prepared to survive this whole ordeal than any of you."

"Maybe it should be our genius pilot over here who landed half the state short of the runway!" spat Asheliegh.

"It was an engine malfunction," pleaded Knox, "we lost both and there was no way for us to make it."

"What about Sully? Huh?" said Karen, "he landed his bird in the Hudson without engines like he did it as a hobby on the weekends. What about that? No lakes around here captain?" said Karen.

"You don't understand, we were falling too fast. Not to mention, my landing saved all your lives, so you're welcome."

"Oh yeah, let's all bow down to the guy who just flew our plane into a mountain," said Asheliegh.

"Captain Knox is right," said Moore, "he killed everyone else but he did, technically, save us."

"What about Karen," continued Mike Moore, "I don't see what Karen here is bringing to the table. She would feed us for a month."

"Honey, you don't want any of this," said Karen, facing the group, "I am 90% high-fructose corn syrup and grease. One bite of me and your teeth will fall out and your heart will stop."

"Okay," said Knox, stepping to the middle of the circle, "we can't eat Mike because if we eat a 'disabled person' it will make us look bad and ruin any chance of going viral. We can't eat Karen because she is, in her own words, disgusting."

Karen shook her head in agreement.

"And we can't eat me because I'm the one who saved us," Said Captain Knox, "so it looks like it's Asheliegh."

"She looks stringy," complained Karen, looking Asheliegh up and down, "there's no meat on her."

"The whole point of this is to go viral," said Asheliegh, "if you eat me, none of you Boomers will know how to get the video out there for the world to see. I'm an influencer. I have 8,000 followers. We'll be instantly famous if I post the video to my account."

"Is 8,000 really an influencer?" asked Karen, "that seems a bit...low."

"Well the brands that ask me to promote their products on my account don't seem to think so," said Asheliegh.

"What kind of brands are we talking about?" Knox asked. "Are we talking like local brands or national campaigns?"

Asheliegh hesitated for a second.

"I mean, like, real brands like...Mary Kay," said Asheliegh, turning away from the group as she mumbled the name.

"Mary Kay is a scam!" said Karen, "I have boxes of their shit in my garage right now! That pyramid scheme cost me a goddamn fortune!"

"What does your profile look like?" Mike Moore asked looking back at Asheliegh, "Is it just bikini pictures and duck-face selfies?"

"No, that's, like, so lame you assume that," Asheliegh replied, taking a moment to pull her jacket closer around her neck to protect against the cold, "it shows...it...it celebrates the female figure and female confidence and stands up to the patriarchy!"

"Oh God, 100 dollars says your followers are all bots and old divorced men. Not a quality following, doesn't count," Mike Moore said.

"My following actually is quality, but, whatever. If you eat me you still won't know how to get the video to go viral, I doubt any of you could open a PDF. Good luck picking the right hashtags."

"I just flew a plane, I think I know how to open a PDF," said Knox, looking over at the wreckage of flight AA79.

"I think my Platinum Pro status speaks for itself," said Mike Moore.

Karen hesitated for a moment. "...Fair enough, yeah, my daughter usually does the fancy technology stuff for me," said Karen, "but I don't see that as a good reason to eat me."

The sound of the buffeting wind of a helicopter interrupted their arguing. In the distance, they could see the beam of a search light bouncing through the sky, scanning the ground as it went.

"They found us," said Asheliegh, as she opened the camera on her phone and pressed record.

"Maybe, this really was all for nothing," said Mike Moore as he opened his mouth wide to flex his jaw.

"As they say, fame takes a perfect combination of timing, patience, execution and a whole lotta luck," said Captain Knox as he popped his knuckles and took a step closer to the group.

"We had our shot. Maybe next time," said Karen, licking her lips and scanning each of the other three up and down.

***

From the air, the search party in the helicopter spotted the pile of survivors in their place a hundred meters from the wreck.

"We got survivors guys!" said the pilot of the helicopter over his shoulder to the other members of his team.

As the rescuers got closer, they looked in awe through their windows at the rat's nest of ligaments jostling in the snow below: Knox had Karen's leg in his mouth who, in turn, was nipping at the small of Asheliegh's back. Mike Moore had Knox's arm by the teeth while he fought off Asheliegh who held a camera in one hand and Mike Moore's ankle with the other.

"What're they doing?" yelled the co-pilot over the radio.

"Man, I don't know," said the helicopter captain. "But take out your phone and record it, this could go super viral."

Daryl

Maeve Goodrich

Daryl was a dog. Not a fun little magical sidekick, not a metaphor for man's essential animal nature, not a princess and the frog style lover, an actual dog: overly large, exceedingly wooly, and of ambiguous parentage. If it hadn't been for his charm Daryl might not have been the man for the job. He was a good guy, Darryl was, he'd never meant to get mixed up in this business.

Daryl was a red-blooded American, born and raised on the streets of Chicago, that windy city, and he knew that it was free-market capitalism that made the world go round. As his father Carl used to say, "Remember son, men are dicks, but it's rational economic actors acting in the own self-interest that price goods and services most efficiently."

Darryl's father managed to die very efficiently of ringworm and exposure after the 2008 recession, when their former owners could no longer afford a set of overlarge, over-hungry dogs. It's not as if the Smiths just threw them out onto the street; it was worse than that. They shipped Daryl and his father to upstate New York to live with Great Aunt Martha, who sucked. She had undiagnosed dementia and an untreated superiority complex, so she sometimes left the dogs outside for two to three days at a time, just for kicks.

Carl couldn't handle the heat, and he died. Daryl ran away, made it to the big apple with his father's last words ringing in his floppy teenaged ears: "Remember son, men are dicks."

The business was armed robbery and Daryl knew the drill. He was a professional working with a group of professionals. They were all devoted to the same cause, a nobly updated Robinhood principle: steal from the rich and keep the money for yourself. "It's better for the economy" the lead dick, Hugh, would say on occasion. Daryl would've called bullshit, bitten Hugh's leg or something, because Daryl was, as I say, a good guy, but he was just trying to get back on his feet, and that was hard enough as a single dog in New York.

The thing about Daryl is that he had excellent posture—this made passers-by trust him. Good posture meant good breeding, and good breeding meant no crime. A dignified dog sitting by an alley, especially a large one like Daryl, garnered just enough attention for people to give him a wide bert—a large hound on the street is generally avoided. Rarely, when someone was suspicious enough to approach the dark alley beside which Daryl proudly sat, he'd thump his tail and slobber retiringly, and the person would pat him and walk away, mollified. Daryl was the lion at the gates of the library, the handsome gargoyle guarding medieval rooftops, the lookout for 27 major heists and counting. He was technically a felon, if dogs can be charged with felonies.

Daryl wasn't sure, but he hoped not.

A WRITER'S EVENING PRAYER

Damilola Oyedele

Made in your likeness, Creator,

I offer this tribute. My throne

is the ninety-degree angle of an L-shaped couch

on whose soft-sharp edge I am

perched; back straight, ankles crossed

royally, room covered in night save

for the brightness of this screen

and backlit keys clicking, clicking

in a soothing rhythm.

Accept the sacrifice from this altar

made of a MacBook Air balanced on my lap

and first thoughts penciled into a lime green journal

now tossed to the side.

From here incense rises, and

my heart, a shining sun

chants with childlike cheer:

"We are praying,

close your eyes,

put your hands to keyboard,

say your prayers".

Electric Luminaire

Art by Lorri Frisbee

Poetry by Leslie D. Soule

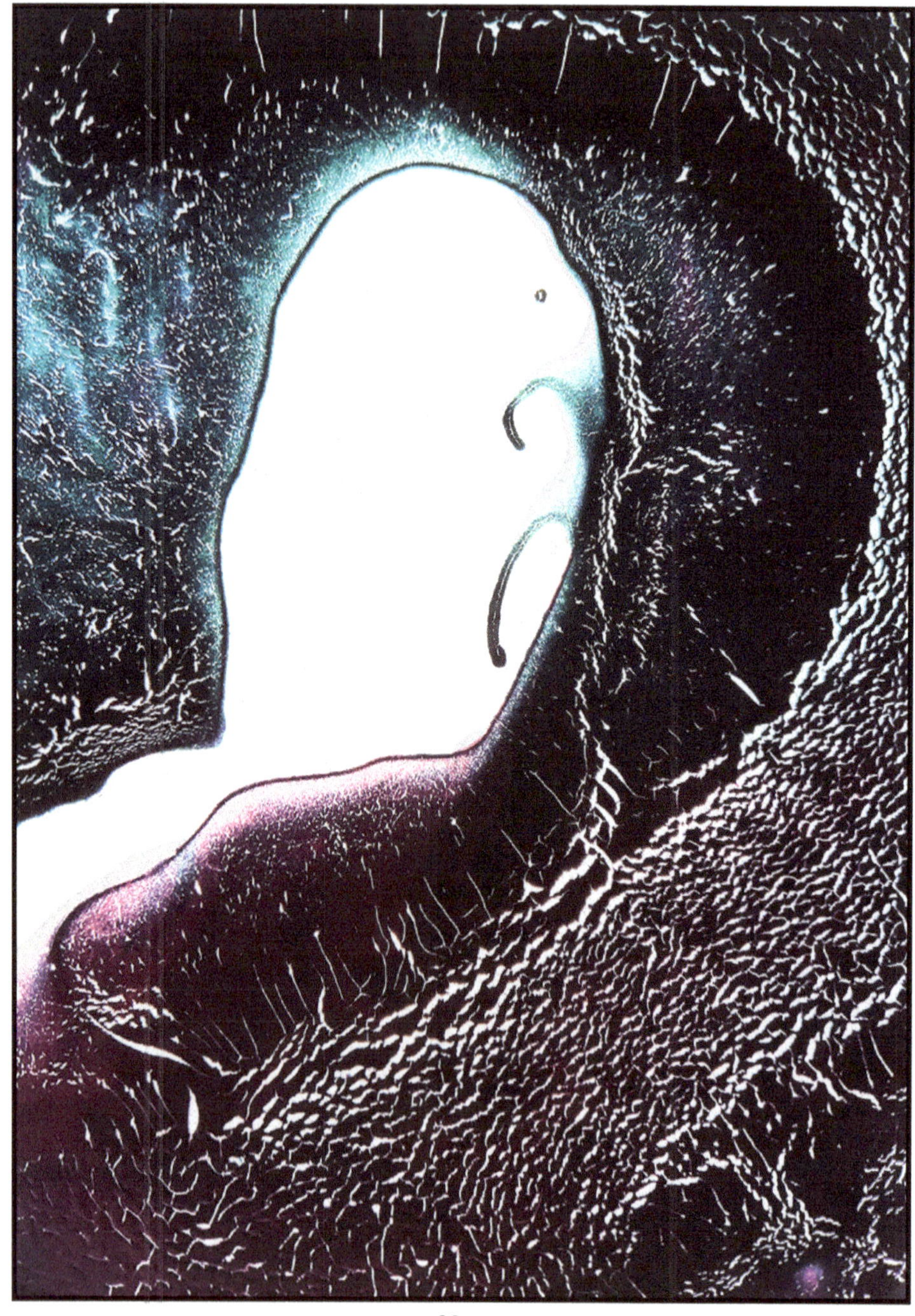

Like a portal to another world

It came crashing through the underdark

Sizzling blue and purple current

With potentialities of green and pink

It ripples, shivers,

Waves eddies of fire and sparks out into force fields

And I saw the shivering shape

Of your actual soul –

Glowing, electric luminaire

In Order Of Appearance:

A. Pikovsky is a poet living in Philly who is the child of Jewish Soviet immigrants. @Little_Windmil

D.T. Graber lives and works in two places--Colorado's Front Range and Tennessee's South Cumberland Plateau--a situation that produces regular road trips between the two. When traveling otherwise, he tends to find himself in places that have been abandoned, if not in places of abandonment. He finds it easiest--or maybe most revealing--to document humanity by the scenes and objects it leaves behind, by accident or with conviction. He likes images of desolation when that desolation speaks.

Brian Baker is a poet living in London, Ontario. He has had poetry published in the University of Windsor Review, the Antigonish Review and Dandelion. As well, he was Poetry London's 2020 winner of the Open Theme Poetry Contest. During the day, he is a support worker involved with intellectually challenged adults. Retirement awaits, in short order!

George Yatchisin is the author of Feast Days (Flutter Press 2016) and The First Night We Thought the World Would End (Brandenburg Press 2019). His poems have been published in journals including Antioch Review, Askew, and Zocalo Public Square. He is co-editor of the anthology Rare Feathers: Poems on Birds & Art (Gunpowder Press 2015), and his poetry appears in the anthologies including Reel Verse: Poems About the Movies (Everyman's Library 2019).
@gyatchisin

Chris Norcross is a Philadelphia based Artist and musician. His work has appeared in various journals, including Chaleur Magazine, ICEVIEW, and Slow Time. His current project explores the fragile status of personal orientation.

Dion Farquhar has poems in Blind Field, Mortar, Birds Piled Loosely, Local Nomad, Columbia Poetry Review, Shampoo, moria, Shifter, BlazeVOX, etc. Her second poetry book Wonderful Terrible was published by Main Street Rag Publishing in 2013, her second chapbook Snap came out in 2017 at Crisis Chronicles Press, and her third chapbook Just Kidding was published by Finishing Line Press in 2018. She works as an exploited adjunct at two universities, but still loves the classroom, and she is active in the University of California Santa Cruz adjunct union, the UC-AFT.

Shyla Shehan is an analytical Virgo who has spent the majority of her life in the Midwest. She holds an MFA in Writing from the University of Nebraska where she received an American Academy of Poets Prize in 2020. Her work has appeared or is forthcoming in Plainsongs, Gyroscope Review, Wild Roof Journal, and her chapbook, "Unsuspecting Cinderella," will be released November 2021. Shyla is the co-founder and EIC of The Good Life Review and currently lives in Omaha, Nebraska with her husband, children, and four cats. All this and more at shylashehan.com.

Alana was born and raised in Staten Island, N.Y. She earned a BA in English at the University of Albany, (NY, 2015). Working in Sales for a camera company in New York City, she takes advantage of their resources as a freelance Photographer. She has hosted her own art show as well as displayed work in Harlem galleries. Prior photographic work has been published online for Hamptons Magazine, and the Snobette. She currently lives in NYC with her dog, Doug and boyfriend, Jeff.
Find her on Instagram: @theartfulspotter

Chelsi Sayti is a third year MFA poet with the University of Nevada, Las Vegas. Her work appears in jubilat, BAG Magazine, and Hey, I'm Alive.

Nikki Raitz is an emerging artist from Atlanta, Georgia whose work has been shown regionally, nationally and internationally. Her body of work focuses on transitory concepts such as dreams, in-between spaces, consciousness and non-tangible notions like trust. Her art communicates a romantic view of subjects by employing dramatic lighting, movement and a sense of mystery. Though she is

classically trained as an oil-painter, Raitz's portfolio includes illustrations, photography, installation art and mural work.
Dance, music and classical literature are a strong influence on her work: dance especially being highlighted throughout her photographic works and pattern being a strong influence in her paintings and illustrations. Her portfolio is constantly expanding as she explores new creative interests, mediums and concepts in unexpected ways. Raitz plans to continue working prosperously across multiple areas of the art field in coming years.
@nikkiraitz

Tom Skove assists his wife, a silk artist, as a photographer. He graduated from Amherst College and Case Western Reserve School of Law. He lives in Cleveland, Ohio.

Eric Braman is an enthusiastic and passionate writer whose work explores themes of nature, Queer identity, masculinity, and mental health. They sit with the intersection of these themes, questioning the foundations of toxic masculinity, exploring the realm of queer possibility, and embodying the self as a element of nature and vice versa. Their work has been published in The Coachella Review and the poetry anthology "Sh!t Men Say to Me" by Moon Tide Press, as well as performed on the collaborative album "By Your Side" with musician Cullen Vance.

Eva Swiecki is a Chicago writer. She is a co-creator of the writing critique group Study Hall Workshops, and has been published in Lammergeier, Wild Roof Journal, and Hooligan Magazine. When she isn't writing, she's at home rearranging the furniture. You can find her on Twitter and her blog, http://brickandhiss.blogspot.com/.

Portland-based photographer/multimedia artist Eric Walker explores the vernacular of signage amongst the American West in the series 'If A Stop Sign Falls' focusing less on the literal directive of the object and more on how it shapes and informs surrounding landscapes. The work aims to hone in on the fragile border between human development and natural processes. Instagram: @edubyeah

Lara Henneman writes fiction, essays, and poetry. Her work is featured or upcoming in McSweeney's Internet Tendency, Sky Island Journal, Baltimore's Child, Scary Mommy, and various Medium publications. She is currently working on her first novel. She has a BA from Brown University and an MA from the University of Denver School of International Studies. She lives in Maryland with her growing family. Find her on Twitter @lhenpen or join her reader list at www.larahenneman.com.

Joseph Fisher is an American expat living in Berlin, Germany. His other work can be found published at Across the Margin, From Whispers to Roars, High Shelf Press, and Wanderlust Travel Journal.

Maeve Goodrich is a struggling college student and aspiring banjoist. She's been published in precious few places but believes she can worm her way into a few more honorable establishments before the day is done.
Her Instagram handle is @maevegoodrich

Damilola Oyedele is a writer whose work explores identity, belonging, and representation. Her essays and criticism have appeared in Brittle Paper, The Mantle, and elsewhere. She is an alumna of Catapult's 12-Month Novel Generator, Hedgebrook Vortext, and the Fidelity Bank Creative Writing Workshop. Damilola lives in Austin, Texas.

Lorri Frisbee has lived all over the world, from Pusan, Korea to Zacatecas, Mexico. She started dreaming of her world travels as a child living in small town Montana. She currently resides in Denver, Colorado and has shown at the Lakewood Cultural Center, the Arvada Cultural Center, The Spark Gallery, The Lapis Gallery, and the Anam Cara Gallery. Her website is lorrifrisbee.com where you can view her multi-media paintings and photography. Her Instagram account is @SIZLfactory.

Leslie D. Soule is a fantasy author who recently completed her Fallenwood Chronicles 4-book series. She holds an M.A. from National University, and is a citizen journalist.

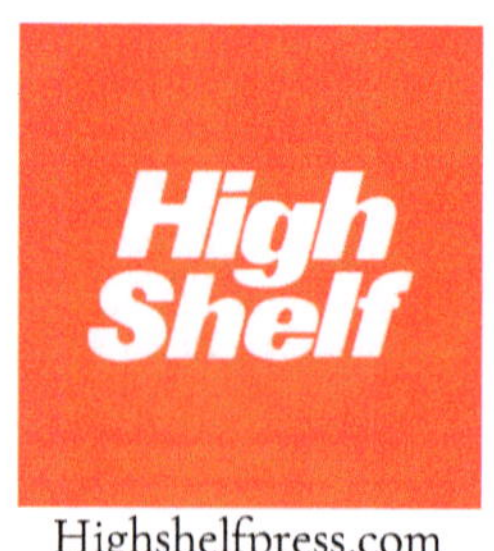

Highshelfpress.com